THE WEST'S
LAST
CHANCE

THE WEST'S
LAST
CHANCE

Will We Win the Clash of Civilizations?

TONY BLANKLEY

Since 1947
REGNERY
PUBLISHING, INC.
An Eagle Publishing Company • Washington, DC

Library of Congress Cataloging-in-Publication Data
Blankley, Tony.

The West's last chance : will we win the clash of civilizations? / Tony Blankley.
p. cm.

Includes bibliographical references and index.

ISBN 0-89526-015-8

1. Civilization, Western—Islamic influences. 2. Islam—Europe. 3. Islam—21st century. 4. Islam and world politics. 5. Terrorism—Religious aspects—Islam. 6. Islamic fundamentalism. 7. Islam—Relations. I. Title.

CB251.B58 2005

813'.6—dc22
2005018259

Published in the United States by
Regnery Publishing, Inc.
One Massachusetts Avenue, NW
Washington, DC 20001
www.regnery.com

Distributed to the trade by
National Book Network
Lanham, MD 20706

Manufactured in the United States of America

10 9 8 7 6 5 4 3 2 1

Books are available in quantity for promotional or premium use. Write to Director of Special Sales, Regnery Publishing, Inc., One Massachusetts Avenue, NW, Washington, DC 20001, for information on discounts and terms, or call (202) 216-0600.

To my parents, Jack and Trixie Blankley,
who were Londoners during World War II,
saw Europe threatened, redeemed to freedom,
and now in the twilight of their years, again threatened.
May their grandchildren live to see the second redemption.

Just as this book was going to press, London was attacked—presumably by Islamist terrorists. With trains and a bus blown up and scores of casualties, the newspapers are filled with the proud, defiant words of Londoners and British government officials. We can only hope those words are followed by actions. But if the complacent mentalities described in this book, which have followed previous such attacks, reemerge, I fear graver, more ferocious terrorist assaults will come before the West takes decisive action.

Contents

Chapter One   *The Nightmare Scenario* 1

Chapter Two   *Hope and Determination* 21

Chapter Three   *The Threat* 35

Chapter Four   *Europe Reacts* 69

Chapter Five   *The Deracination of the West* 95

Chapter Six   *Saving Democracy, 1940s Style* 107

Chapter Seven   *A World in Transition* 133

Chapter Eight   *The Way Forward* 161

Acknowledgments 199

Bibliography 201

Notes 205

Index 219

The Nightmare Scenario

London, England
March 15, 2007

O N A DREARY SPRING DAY IN LONDON, preaching outside a Finsbury Park mosque to a crowd that numbered no more than a few dozen, a Moroccan cleric called for the British government to end the public display of sacrilegious art. The initial target of his campaign was the aluminum statue of a nude Eros atop the bronze fountain at Piccadilly Circus.

He could easily have picked any of dozens of statues on the streets or parks of London. But his choice of Piccadilly Circus was shrewd. Five traffic arteries intersect at the roundabout in central London and could be easily disrupted by street protesters. Nearby Underground stations gave protesters easy means to converge on or disperse from the targeted site. In Hyde Park or a quiet square, the protesters would scarcely be noticed. But at Piccadilly they would be highly visible, and their potential for creating mayhem could escalate the protests to a new level of disruption.

The cleric liked to think of this as "scalability." His plan was to see the protests rise first in England, and then across Europe, where the growing Muslim *ummah* (the people of Islam) was forced to live under the most impure conditions.

Piccadilly Circus was the logical starting place for his jihad to cover up offensive art. The fountain had become world-famous during the 1960s, ranking alongside Carnaby Street as one of "swinging London's" defining landmarks. It had become a must-see destination for millions of tourists annually. It epitomized the decadence Islamists so detested in the societies they had chosen to inhabit.

At first, the authorities tolerated the protests. The Metropolitan Police confined their vigilance to cordoning off the sidewalks and keeping the protesters from disrupting traffic. But as the cleric had foreseen, the protests caused rubbernecking motorists to slow down, jamming traffic flows throughout the West End. The media coverage was global. For weeks editorialists wrote angrily on the topic in newspapers, while television talk shows were inflamed with the pros and cons of whether liberal democracies should allow the display of artwork that offends religious sensibilities.

The authorities tried to minimize the disruption by limiting permits for the protests to off-peak traffic hours. But the cleric simply called on observant Muslims to disregard the new restrictions and congregate during rush hour. This civil disobedience gave pundits another twist on the debate and breathed new life into the editorials and talk shows.

There was another debate under way, parallel in many respects to the media debate but unknown to most. This debate raged in Arabic-language Internet chat rooms, on websites, at Friday prayer sessions in mosques, and wherever two or more Muslim men gathered in Europe for tea and cigarettes.

The parallel discussion focused more on the tactics used by the Piccadilly protesters than on the legitimacy of their goals. While many Muslims were deeply troubled by the actions of the radicals, their voices did not dominate. In fact, their voices were largely absent, especially after the mysterious killing of a prominent Muslim lecturer at the London School of Economics.

The lecturer was known as an advocate of restraint. Worried about adding to the growing tensions, the Metropolitan Police kept news of the killing to a minimum by simply making one brief announcement that an academic had been found dead in his flat. No details were provided. There was no mention in the British press of the slit throat or that the victim was a Muslim.

But rumors swept through the Arabic-language websites. In that parallel debate, restraint for its own sake was no longer a topic of advocacy. The only question raised was whether the nonviolent protests would be sufficient to rid European society of its addiction to vice.

But the parallel debate was largely ignored in the media. Some British intellectuals expressed sympathy for the protesters, arguing that a culturally tolerant society could not allow forms of expression that were abominable to Muslims or other significant minority groups. These arguments were fiercely countered by the country's cultural and artistic elites, who warned that any restriction of publicly funded art on religious grounds would inevitably lead to unadulterated censorship.

Public sympathy swung against the Muslim protesters when they became violent. The first riot broke out when a protester recognized a curator from the Tate Modern and called for her car to be blocked. The curator had briefly achieved media notoriety in Britain's tabloids for her involvement in a major retrospective of biomorphism. The exhibit, which featured the sexual content of the movement's artwork, had outraged many conservative Britons.

Although some say the curator had been covertly targeted by the Islamic extremists—who knew her route home, had photographed her car, and had given the photo to the protest organizers—what happened next might have been spontaneous. A crowd gathered around the car and began rocking it violently before breaking the windows and dragging the woman and her husband into the street, where they found themselves surrounded and unable to escape. When another motorist tried to drive into the crowd to aid the frightened couple, several protesters were knocked down. A full-scale riot broke out. Motorists stuck in the snarled traffic around Piccadilly were dragged from their cars and badly beaten. Cars were set ablaze, and the Metropolitan Police needed large numbers of reinforcements before the demonstrators could be brought under control.

As the cleric had hoped, the incident was the perfect catalyst. Islamic supporters who had previously confined themselves to Internet ranting or coffee-shop chatter swung into action.

In Italy, a small bomb planted at night destroyed Little David, the copy of Michelangelo's masterpiece that stands in a public square in Florence. A communication from the bomber taking credit for the attack cited the statue as doubly offensive to Muslim standards, for it was not only a statue, but a nude one, and was therefore in violation of Muslim prohibitions against nudity. In Rome, a man tried unsuccessfully to bomb Antonio Canova's nude marble of Pauline Bonaparte as Venus in the Borghese Gallery. While pundits smugly opined that perhaps the Florentine bomber was unaware that the real David was safely confined inside the Gallerie dell'Accademia, the incidents nonetheless caused authorities to reassess the vulnerability of museums and publicly displayed artwork to attack or vandalism. Across the country, museums were shut down pending security reviews. Most metropolitan museums, such as the Uffizi in Florence, were able to reopen within days;

precautions against domestic terrorist groups like the Red Brigades had been in place long before Islamic terrorism reached Europe. But in smaller towns, many provincial museums were unable to reopen for months until they could extensively upgrade their security.

In Spain, a fanatic used acid to attack Albrecht Dürer's sixteenth-century paintings of Adam and Eve, considered to be the finest example of German Renaissance figure painting not just in the Museo del Prado but in the world. Although the nudes were modestly painted with leaves from the apple tree covering their genitals, they were nonetheless acutely offensive to Muslim extremists. The artist's portrayal of the first man and woman made by the hand of God was considered the ultimate effrontery.

Greater vigilance at French museums made an outright attack on the Louvre or the Beaubourg impractical. The French gendarmerie, made up disproportionately of recruits from rough provinces far from the Métropole, such as Corsica, took no chances. The tough provincials intimidated Muslim males. So instead of targeting museums, small squads of hooded Muslims ransacked undefended commercial art galleries in a coordinated series of raids throughout Paris. Sparing landscapes and abstract art, they destroyed antique and contemporary artwork featuring the human body and smashed statuary. French insurance officials estimated the damages of the day at thirty million euros. In an attempt to destroy Auguste Rodin's *The Kiss*, a larger-than-life marble statue of a nude man and woman embracing in an ardent kiss, a car bomb was detonated outside the Musée Auguste Rodin in Paris. The attempt breached the building slightly but failed to destroy the statue. Several schoolchildren passing nearby were killed, and dozens of Parisians of all ages were injured.

In editorial columns in the following weeks, well-meaning Muslim intellectuals and artists deplored the actions of the extremists. But it was too late to contain the contagion. Over the next few months, literally thousands of statues in public places across the breadth of Europe were ruined. The vandalism was unprecedented. Nothing had done so much damage to Europe's cultural heritage since the widespread destruction of the Second World War.

In an effort to safeguard statuary, municipalities began removing artwork from public places. They were put—temporarily, it was hoped—into secure storage for safekeeping. Curiously, artwork in churches was left unharmed. The consensus of the imams in the Internet chat rooms and in the mosques was that Christians ought to be allowed to worship as they pleased, even if their churches and cathedrals contained idols.

This degree of tolerance mirrored the rule of Islam in Spain during the seven hundred-year span between the eighth and fifteenth centuries. Spain's Mohammedan conquerors never required Christians or Jews to convert to Islam. In fact, the caliphs preferred that many of the peoples they conquered remain non-believers, because the Koran permitted the faithful to extract tribute from infidels. The Jews and Christians who retained their original faith were heavily taxed, and the revenue they gave under duress sustained the Muslim expansion. In exchange, the Christians and Jews were allowed to keep their places of worship and their traditions, including artistic traditions.

But art on display in public places, and at public expense, was a different matter. The British government was the first to form a blue-ribbon commission to explore the public policy dimensions of the problem. The commission was composed of an amalgam of politicians, cultural intellectuals, and religious authorities drawn from a range of faiths, including Islam. Its charter was to explore the limits to which artists and intellectuals should be permitted to create works that offended the religious sensibilities of any group, especially a marginalized group or minority.

The British example was quickly followed by the establishment of similar commissions in competing European power centers, notably Germany and France. Brussels came next, when the European Union established an official commission. Within a few months, every European country except Switzerland and Norway had established a commission on religious, artistic, and cultural expression.

The results of these deliberations were presented as a reasonable series of compromises. Permanent, multi-denominational commissions were established to review current and proposed artwork in public venues, with a view toward removal of those considered offensive to the public taste, or to a substantial minority of the public. Many of the statues that had been removed from public streets for protective reasons never reappeared. In their place, municipalities put abstract statuary, including new works freshly commissioned from Muslim artists.

Most museums were reorganized so that Muslims could enter and view works of interest, such as landscapes and Islamic exhibits, without being exposed to idolatrous or sacrilegious art. In the process, many secondary paintings, primarily of interest to scholars and connoisseurs, were simply never rehung or displayed. They quietly disappeared into storage, where only serious researchers were permitted to see them.

Some extremists remained unsatisfied with these measures. They pressed for further restrictions, with separate days for men and women to attend museums and cultural events. But they were, for the time being, in the minority and were initially unable to achieve their demands.

Ironically, the statue of Eros in Piccadilly Circus, where the protest movement had begun, was left intact under the exemption for religiously inspired art. It so happened that the statue had been originally erected in the nineteenth century in honor of Lord Shaftesbury, a prominent philanthropist who was considered an exemplar of Christian charity.

Once apprised of this overlooked purpose, the cleric who had originally called for the protests conceded that a monument to charity was acceptable, provided the nude Eros could be covered. Folds of cloth wrought in aluminum were carefully crafted and appropriately placed, and the statue remained atop the bronze fountain.

The cleric was satisfied. He had, after all, achieved his true purpose. What was one statue, more or less, when the streets of Europe had been cleansed of thousands of offensive works of art?

While Europe grappled with the Islamist challenge to her artistic heritage, across the Atlantic, the United States was in the middle of yet another very close race for the presidency. After six years, the Republican Party's claim that it had protected America from terrorist attacks since September 11, 2001, had finally been contradicted.

On September 11, 2007, a string of simultaneous Islamist bomb blasts struck big suburban shopping malls in Pennsylvania, Michigan, Ohio, and California. While the deaths from those blasts—about 1,500 killed and 7,000 wounded—were fewer than in 2001, the fact that they happened in suburbia rather than in New York or Washington shocked many Americans.

Some analysts said the Republicans' rhetoric about taking the war to the terrorists in distant countries like Afghanistan and Iraq had back-fired, because it lured people into an unwarranted sense of security at home. Others said that the Department of Homeland Security's incomprehensible alert system and previous false alarms had lulled average Americans into complacency. Realists simply observed that six years without a major terrorist attack was a significant accomplishment, but it was inevitable that with so many potential targets, porous borders, and an intelligence system that still hadn't penetrated radical Islamist cells, sooner or later the terrorists would strike again.

Public outrage over the attacks was compounded by the timid rescue tactics of the police, firefighters, and paramedics. Trained, since 2001, to wait for bomb squads to provide an all-clear against secondary explosives—bombs timed to go off after an initial explosion draws crowds and emergency personnel to the scene—they waited as long as forty-five minutes before attending to the wounded in some sections of the mall in Ohio. The robotic bomb-detection equipment funded by Homeland Security was inadequate for the wreckage and debris it had to deal with and gave a false positive, registering the presence of explosive materials that turned out to be residue from the blast. In the delay, a twelve-year-old girl and her eight-year-old brother bled to death in full view of one of the only mall security cameras still capturing video. Authorities tried to prevent the tape's broadcast, but a purloined copy was furnished to al Jazeera, and from there it went to American television, where it played incessantly in the week following the bombings.

Democratic and Republican primary candidates raced to meet with officials and visit hospitals where victims were undergoing treatment. This bought them time to wait for overnight polls that would give them a gauge on how to respond to the outrages.

Unlike the Spanish in 2003, the American public in 2007 reacted sternly to the renewed violence. Pollsters in both parties found widespread support for extreme measures to contain the Islamist threat. By the time the presidential primaries had ended, both the Republican and the Democratic nominees had taken strong positions.

What followed was one of the strangest twists in American presidential politics in history. It not only turned the presidential contest upside down, but also inadvertently created unprecedented upheaval in Europe.

The Democratic candidate for president was yet another senator from New England. She was determined not to be seen as weak by an electorate that wanted blood. In an attempt to one-up the Republican candidate, she came out in favor of registration and curfew requirements for all Muslims in the United States, even those who were American citizens.

Her position, announced in a major speech on the first anniversary of the September 11 shopping mall bombings, naturally inflamed the passions of American Muslims. They took to the streets in peaceful but massive protest.

The Republican candidate had for years been secretly uneasy with President George W. Bush's confrontational approach in the Middle East. That, in fact, became his main selling point in the Republican primaries. As the suicide bombings in Iraq continued to kill and maim American servicemen, the moderate wing of the GOP successfully positioned him to take advantage of "Iraq fatigue." He was the candidate who would bring our troops home, improve relations with our allies, and soften the Republican image for the 2008 election. But in the immediate aftermath of the mall bombings, his voice had been among the most strident of the Republican primary candidates. As the months after the bombings passed without another terrorist incident, he had tried to mitigate his counter-terrorist position. He returned to his "recapture the middle ground" strategy, beginning with an inclusive and optimistic acceptance speech at the Republican National Convention.

Now his challenger was outrunning him on an important issue with a policy proposal he believed to be unconstitutional. Worse still, he had been caught completely unaware. None of his crack campaign staff had warned him.

Where was the opposition research? Why hadn't his press secretary picked up on the customary rumblings of the news media and tidbits of background that always preceded a big development in a presidential campaign? Sometimes it seemed that he was the only one paying close attention to the race, that his staff and aides had grown too complacent, even arrogant, during eight years of GOP rule. Many were too young to remember the years when Republicans had been in the minority in Congress and had had to fight hard not only to win the White House but also even to govern with an opposition party in Congress. These younger Republicans had developed a sense of entitlement, he thought.

He sensed a political opportunity in his Democratic opponent's announcement. A Republican insider who had recently signed on to his campaign had been building bridges between American Muslim voters and Republican politicians for more than a decade. The adviser thought of himself as one of the few campaign strategists who took the long view of politics. He believed that Arab American votes were the key to offsetting the Democratic Party's traditional heavy support among American Jewish voters.

In a hastily convened campaign strategy session, the adviser argued passionately for the Republican candidate to seize the moment to reach out to Muslims. But the campaign's pollster urged caution until more data was available. She pointed out that in focus groups held before the conventions, suburban mothers had voiced strong support for any candidate who would do whatever necessary to protect their children's safety, even if it meant internment camps or forced repatriation for Muslims. Taking a strong stand against Islamic radicalism will resonate with women, the pollster kept saying. But because she had no specific recommendation of what sort of "strong stand" would work—and wouldn't look like he was merely copying his Democratic opponent with me-tooism—her counsel was disregarded.

The Republican contender decided to take a bold gamble. It was, he thought, one of those rare moments in a presidential election campaign when good policy and good politics coincided. The polls consistently had shown the race to be about even at 48 percent to 48 percent, with 4 percent undecided. But Muslims were over-represented within the unde-cided category. Although usually reliable Democratic voters, under the circumstances the Muslim vote looked gettable for a sympathetic Repub-lican senator who had never been strongly supportive of President Bush.

Among the states that were too close to call were Michigan, Ohio, and New Jersey, which also had some of the highest numbers of Mus-lim voters. Ohio and New Jersey had about fifty thousand Muslims, Michigan about thirty thousand. (California and New York had more Muslim voters but were safe Democratic states.) With a strong get-out-the-vote effort and a potentially lopsided support for one candidate, the Muslim vote could decide the contest in all three states. It was con-ventional wisdom that the candidate who carried two of those three states would win the presidency. The Republican thought that by advo-cating a curfew and registration policy for Muslims, the Democratic nominee had just handed him the keys to the White House.

But first he had to take action. He brushed off his pollster, saying he didn't have the luxury of time to wait on further polling data. He told his press secretary to inform the networks, on background, that he would soon be responding to his opponent's proposal on curfew and registration. He had his manager contact the organizers of a Muslim rally in Trenton, New Jersey, to arrange for him to address the crowd.

He warned his staff that aside from giving background to the net-works, he wanted no leaks—not a word to Matt Drudge, no blogging, no Washington Whispers—until the morning of his speech. He wanted to build suspense and interest. "I don't want the air leaking out of the balloon," he said.

That same day, his advance team rushed to Philadelphia, rented cars, and drove to Trenton to plan the event. They failed to foresee the size of the crowd that turned out, and the candidate's motorcade had trouble getting to the rally, which was at the Sovereign Bank Arena on South Broad Street near the state capitol building in Trenton. The arena seated only ten thousand people, and the fire marshal had, hours before, officially declared the building already well beyond capacity and closed it to any further entrants. The streets between the capitol and the arena were jammed with Muslims who couldn't get in. The candidate's motorcade was stuck.

Looking out the smoked windows of the campaign's Suburban, he saw the growing crowd and signs bobbing up and down that read: CURFEW NO. SHARIA YES!

He thought back to his trip to England before the campaign. He had met with the British Muslim Council, which had told him that 60 percent of British Muslims wanted to be governed by Islamic *sharia* law rather than British Common Law. Sharia is the broad collection of laws compiled over a thousand years of Muslim jurisprudence and is based on the Koran and its commentaries, the Sunnah or Hadith. While the British government had turned down the request, several British members of Parliament told him the government was considering the idea.

By the time he reached the arena, he was about an hour late. He hurried to the microphone on stage and was met with wild applause. That morning's Drudge Report had predicted that the Muslim audience would like what it was going to hear. Text messages had reverberated among cell phones for hours, and the crowd was in a frenzy of anticipation.

He was about five minutes into his speech when he delivered his big line: He would vote against the curfew law when it came up in the Senate. That generated only a murmur of polite applause. Clearly, they expected more. Someone in the crowd started chanting "Sharia, sharia, sharia in the USA." The entire arena filled with a rhythmic "sha-ri-a, sha-ri-a, sha-ri-a." The arena thundered to the sound of feet pounding and hands clapping.

The sense of power was intoxicating. The senator was a seasoned politician, but he had never experienced anything quite like this. Although the crowd gave not the slightest indication of unruliness, it was definitely agitated.

His speech was drowned out by the chanting. He waited patiently for his moment to pick up the next line off the teleprompter. The thought crossed his mind that he and his press secretary were the only two Christians in an increasingly impassioned crowd of ten to fifteen thousand Muslims, with perhaps another five to ten thousand immediately outside.

He wasn't exactly afraid. He was too tough an old warhorse for that; he had learned to face down fear as a Marine in Vietnam. But engulfed in the energy of the crowd, and thinking about the polls, the election, the opportunity that might slip out of his hands if he played the next few minutes wrong, he was clearly unsteady, perhaps even unnerved. Few politicians get through a career without misplaying a moment in front of a crowd. But rarely has a politician misjudged such a moment with more consequence.

He was known for being able to work a crowd better than any of his contemporaries, so he always insisted on wearing a radio mike to be free to roam around the stage. *This is my moment*, he thought. *Get physical. Be dramatic. Wrap up the election right now. Bring it all home. No guts, no glory.*

He looked out into the crowd and sensed a slight slackening of energy. An agitated crowd is like a tide—the energy ebbs and flows. He knew how to time the cycle and catch each wave. He pulled off his suit jacket, grabbed the table next to the lectern, dragged it to the edge of the stage, leaped up on it, and threw out his arms to the audience. Giant television screens projected his image to every corner of the arena. The crowd fell miraculously silent.

And then he said: "It's time for sharia in America."

The crowd exploded in ecstasy. When they finally quieted down, he was prepared to make his case to the broader American audience beyond the arena.

"There are only a handful of terrorists. Our challenge is to reduce that number, not expand it. We've been in the Muslims' faces for too long. Of course, all Americans must be law-abiding. But for our Muslim citizens, let the law they abide by be the peaceful law of sharia.

"Sharia," he said, "is a friend of strong family values, and therefore of strong American values."

While the audience erupted in cheers, he thought of another rally he had attended, for a group called Promise Keepers. They were evangelical Christians, and they believed that a father was the rightful head of his family. They believed that it was God's will that a family have a single decision-maker, a father whose authority should be obeyed for the good of the family. Islam's sharia, he thought, wasn't that much different.

He had stumped in Baptist-dominated counties in Florida where alcohol sales were banned and women kept themselves dressed from neck to ankle in public, even at the beach. There is, he thought, a parallel between Islam and the Baptists—though he couldn't think of any examples of organized Baptist violence or terrorism.

Still, he thought, as long as he kept his advocacy of sharia linked to family values, he was all right. The senator wasn't terribly religious, but he was a social conservative. He had long advocated controls on obscenity and indecency in the media, especially in film and television. Republicans and Muslims could agree that Hollywood was Babylon. Republicans and Muslims could be allies in the effort to curb the excesses of the entertainment industry. Republicans and Muslims could stand together against social deviancy.

When he wrapped up his remarks, the crowd was chanting his name. He had played the whole scene perfectly. While many of his staff were white-faced with fear at what the political fallout would be, the senator scoffed, "Listen to that crowd." He hadn't said anything that wasn't already being seriously discussed in Canada and Europe; he had merely taken the lead in America.

At the news of his speech, Muslims in Europe, the Middle East, and Asia were jubilant. In America, the euphoria among Muslims was uncontrollable.

In the next poll taken after the speech, he was getting 92 percent of the Muslim vote. But despite the fact that the Democratic candidate had been a liberal champion of abortion rights and tax increases, the conservative base deserted the Republican Party on the issues of terrorism and sharia. Evangelical Christians, for whom religion was always more important than politics, simply stayed home and didn't vote.

Female voters, already warm to the Democratic nominee's tough position, were doubly angered by the Republican senator's embrace of Muslim causes. Not only was he opposed to measures they thought vital to protect their children, he apparently also wanted women veiled in burkas, stoned for adultery, and required to produce at least four male witnesses before they could file a rape charge with the police. At least that's how Democratic pundits spun the sharia speech in the days following the politically disastrous Trenton appearance.

The final fifty days of the presidential race were a mockery of a real campaign. Polls showed that the race had ended as soon as the Republican endorsed sharia. The Democratic candidate won two-thirds of the women's vote and took the White House with 58 percent of the popular vote. Terrorism had trumped all other issues, just as it had in the elections of 2002 and 2004. After the slaughter in the suburbs, Americans demanded the harshest possible policy against terrorism. No other issue seriously mattered.

But in Europe it went quite the other way. The Republican candidate's call for sharia came just as the European governments were—prudently, in their opinion—conceding to Muslim sensibilities on the public display of art. To Islamists in Europe, the two events confirmed their conviction that the West was decadent, weak, and unwilling to defend itself.

Throughout Arabic-language chat rooms, even moderate Muslims were admitting that the extremists had been right all along—at least when it came to the feasibility of building a dominantly Muslim Europe. Eurabia seemed within their grasp.

A week after the sharia announcement in Trenton, the Muslim councils in Britain, France, Germany, and Holland held a joint meeting in London. These councils, which were usually composed of responsible, relatively moderate, and often prominent Muslim men, had been on the defensive for years. Younger, more radical Muslims in Europe saw them as sellouts to the Crusaders. Their willingness to work with the governments of Europe to advance Muslim conditions and rights was seen as not only insufficiently radical, but as evidence that they were not devout Muslims at all. Their centers and neighborhood meetings were being supplanted by increasingly radicalized conversation on the Internet.

At the extraordinary London meeting, it was quickly agreed that if they were to have any voice in future European affairs, they had to get out in front of the debate. They called on the European Union Parliament in Brussels to immediately designate sharia law as the official law for all Muslims living in EU countries. The EU tabled the topic for discussion in sixty days.

Such was the pitch of excitement among the Muslim communities of the EU that what for Brussels seemed like very fast action was now seen as a delaying tactic and denounced as such by the growing number of Muslim radicals.

Once again, the hooded men came out to bomb. Whereas last time art galleries had been targeted, this time the law courts were in the crosshairs. At first, the terrorists hit only small, unguarded courthouses in provincial towns. But when a suicide truck bomb exploded outside the Old Bailey—London's historic central criminal courthouse—tearing the famous front off the building and causing major damage to St. Paul's Cathedral, two hundred yards up the street, it was just too much.

The dean of St. Paul's held a press conference to announce that engineers had informed him that the great cathedral, which had been built by Sir Christopher Wren in 1675 and had survived six years of Nazi bombing during World War II, would have to be abandoned pending major reconstruction. A funereal mood fell over London after the loss of St. Paul's and the Old Bailey, landmarks of London, of England's history. And in Europe, the will to resist broke.

In Paris the next day, the conservative daily *Le Figaro* ran an unusual five-column headline: "Is the Eiffel Tower Next?" The paper's lead editorial—dryly titled "Each to Their Own"—called for giving the Muslims their sharia law.

In the public housing flats near the docks in Rotterdam, violence broke out. These flats were populated relatively equally by working-class, indigenous Dutch and second- and third-generation Muslims. Tempers had been on edge for years, even before the recent Islamist terrorist strikes. There were two large buildings in the area. One was the Feyenoord soccer stadium, the temple to Dutch soccer and long considered the symbol of the Dutch working class. Built right next door was a nearly completed Muslim mosque designed to seat 1,500 worshippers. Its minarets soared 164 feet into the air. The Rotterdam Dutch were furious that the minarets cast shadows over their beloved soccer stadium.

Three days after the terrible London bombing, a large contingent of Dutch workers stormed the empty mosque and set it afire. Riots broke out that required the Dutch army to intervene. There were rumors on the Internet that some Dutch policemen displayed little interest in stopping the riots, as the Dutch were getting the better of their unwelcome neighbors that night.

In the great European debate that followed, it was noted that the usually tolerant Dutch had not been the same since the assassination of Theo van Gogh back in November 2004, when a radical Muslim had brutally murdered the artist, filmmaker, and distant relative of the great painter Vincent van Gogh. More than a dozen Muslim schools and community centers had been bombed in the weeks after the assassination, and since then, the Dutch had increasingly voted for right-wing candidates.

But most European leaders were not prepared to confront radical Islam. They were not prepared to risk mass violence between Europeans and Muslims. Nor were they prepared to lose any more of the great buildings of Europe to Islamist bombers. They were prepared to make a deal.

After all, Paris and Rome had both been saved during World War II by designating them as open cities. It was time, Europe's leaders thought, to make Europe an open continent—even if it meant giving in to their excitable Muslim populations.

Peace, of a type, was restored during the following month in Brussels. The presidents of the Muslim councils from each of the EU nations negotiated a concordance with the EU government. The presidents would form a Council of Muslim Council Presidents (the now famous CMCP), based in Brussels.

Four conditions were agreed to:

1. The CMCP would have veto power over any EU or EU member state's foreign policy decisions that might affect a Muslim nation.
2. The CMCP would have access to any police investigation of a Muslim, including alleged Muslim terrorists, carried out by the EU, Interpol, or any member state's police or intelligence authority, in order to ensure that Muslim rights were not being infringed upon.
3. The EU would create a commission, which would include the CMCP as a voting member, to institute a regular five-year review of all European laws. Laws that would reasonably give offense to Muslims living in Europe would be repealed.
4. The EU would immediately repeal all anti-immigration laws and procedures that disproportionately limited Muslim immigration to EU countries.

Seventy-two hours after the announcement of the Brussels Concordance, the newly elected Democratic president of the United States asked the Senate to pass a resolution declaring the severance of all ties between United States military, intelligence, and police agencies and the European Union and each of its several members "in the interest of fundamental national security." The resolution was approved by unanimous vote.

The next day the Dow Jones dropped 1,200 points in anticipation of reduced international trade and the probable increase in the price of oil to $200 a barrel.

America braced itself to stand alone.

CHAPTER TWO

Hope and Determination

THAT NIGHTMARE SCENARIO COULD happen. In fact, it could be worse. The threat of the radical Islamists taking over Europe is every bit as great to the United States as was the threat of the Nazis taking over Europe in the 1940s. We cannot afford to lose Europe. We cannot afford to see Europe transformed into a launching pad for Islamist jihad.

My purpose in writing this book is to assess, with cold logic and objectivity, how the West is responding to the radical Islamist threat—and how we can and should respond. My central assertion is that while we in the United States and Europe have vast resources for protecting ourselves, we have thought ourselves into a position of near impotence.

In much of the West, and particularly in Europe, there is a blind denial that radical Islam is transforming the world. Most European elites and far too many American politicians and journalists believe that our challenges are business and politics as usual. They are sheep who cannot sense the wolf pack in the woods; they see the odd wolf tail, but can't imagine wolves' teeth in their throats. Even many who recognize the danger are unable to think outside of "business as usual."

Nevertheless, I am optimistic that America and Europe (and the other outposts of Western civilization around the world) have a very good chance of rallying to defeat this mortal challenge. There are sound reasons to expect that we will preserve our values, culture, and traditions that began to form 1,500 years ago, when the early Christian Church started its great task of converting the barbarians in what came to be called Europe.[1]

The central shortcomings of the West's feeble response, to date, derive from the natural human instinct to forget the distant past and to assume that the more or less benign trends of the recent past will continue. In truth, human history unfolds in dynamic social responses to the present that lead to sudden changes of course. From the extraordinary explosion of Alexander the Great, to the birth of Christ, to the French Revolution, to the American Civil War, to the rise of Hitler, shocking divergences from the status quo have defined the path of history.

King Darius of Persia never imagined—even as he faced Alexander at the Battle of Issus in 333 B.C.—that within three years he would be dead, his Achaemenid Dynasty ended, and the great hegemonic Persian Empire crushed and conquered as a result of that outnumbered Macedonian upstart. American farmers in 1860 never dreamed that within months their husbands, sons, and brothers would be killed in battle and that America would be transformed by continental war. And Londoners in the summer of 1939, my parents included, never expected that forty thousand of their fellow Londoners would soon lie dead in the streets from German bombing, and that within five years Great Britain would never be great again.

There is no more misleading phrase in the English language than "if current trends continue." Stability is an illusion. Change is all. For both individuals and peoples, current trends never continue for very long. We need to grasp the idea of discontinuity. We need to think in terms of when current trends will stop—and what will follow them.

The first discontinuity we must recognize is that the mortal threat we face comes not merely from Osama bin Laden and a few thousand terrorists. Rather, we are confronted with the Islamic world—a fifth of mankind—in turmoil, and insurgent as it has not been in at least five hundred years, if not fifteen hundred years. The magnitude of this cultural upheaval cannot yet be measured. Efforts to count the "jihadist" percentage are pointless, if not dangerously misleading. There is a dynamic process under way that may peter out before it touches one in a hundred Muslims. Or it may impassion a vastly greater number. The latter is far more likely.

Such a force of Muslim energy has not been seen since the rise of the Ottoman Turks in the fifteenth century. In the following two hundred years, that energy overwhelmed Bulgaria, Serbia, Adrianople, Kosovo, most of the rest of the Balkan Peninsula, Constantinople, Budapest, Transylvania, Walachia, Moldavia, Persia, Egypt, Syria, and Greece. Only at the gates of Vienna in 1683 was the surge finally stopped—and then only barely.

Today we face a force of human passion that may well match a similar expansion that burst out of Renaissance Christian Europe and came to be known in the West as the Age of Discovery—but was known everywhere else as the age of conquest, imperialism, and colonialism. And, let it be noted, the quality of the human stock that surged out of fifteenth-century Europe was in no way superior to that which today peoples the Islamic world.

But one must be careful to avoid literalism with historic analogies. History is a guide to human potentialities; it is not necessarily a blueprint or predictor of particular strategies or tactics. The Ottoman Turks rode forth on horseback with curved swords in hand. The energy of Islam today insinuates itself through the forces of globalization and the Internet.

Scholars have long observed that the Protestant Reformation would not have been possible without Gutenberg's invention of movable type. The doctrinal requirement of a direct relation between the Protestant Christian and his Bible (without the intermediation of a church hierarchy) was only possible when Bibles were cheap enough to print that every man, or at least every small village, could afford one. The printing press made that possible. The century-long wars of religion that ensued between Catholic and Protestant armies killed millions of European Christians.

Today, astute observers, such as former senior CIA official Michael Scheuer, are beginning to notice that the worldwide rise of Islamic unrest would not be possible without the Internet. The Internet creates virtual communities of interest. For Islamic terrorists, it is a forum in which they can train in every aspect of terrorism. Such online training renders physical training camps (such as bin Laden set up in Afghanistan only a decade ago, and which we fought a war in 2001 to dismantle) unnecessary.

Similarly, the passion, the propaganda, even the threats and intimidation are only a keystroke away from anyone, Muslim or otherwise, who wants to intellectually engage in the debates that currently roil Islam. According to one count, the number of explicitly terrorist-supporting Internet sites has risen from twelve to over two thousand in only a few years. The number of websites engaged in general Islamic argument and propaganda are too numerous to yet be counted.

Beyond the growing number of Muslims committed to terrorism is the threat from the Islamic diaspora's growing cultural and religious assertiveness—particularly in largely secular Europe, where Muslim cultural assimilation has not occurred.

Curiously, despite (or perhaps because of) America's deeper and more pervasive religious faith and practice, American Muslims have better assimilated into our culture. As befits a nation of immigrants, our culture has always welcomed other peoples more instinctively than have the more ethnically homogeneous European nations. But even in America, the danger of Muslim cultural assertiveness must be monitored and contained.

Europe's problem is compounded by its below-replacement birthrate. Until recently, European elites expected to make up for this potential taxpayer shortfall through immigration, largely from Islamic countries. Now it is beginning to dawn on Europeans that the combination of a shrinking ethnic European population combined with an expanding and culturally assertive Muslim population might lead to the fall of Europe's Western civilization within a century.

This phenomenon, now called Eurabia, is being viewed with growing fatalism both in Europe and in America. Such fatalism, however, is premature. It is precisely on this point that we can be most flagrantly misled by assuming that current trends will continue.

The assassination and butchering of Dutch filmmaker Theo van Gogh (who had made a film revealing Islamic abuse of women) by an Islamist terrorist in November 2004 aroused deep fears in Holland and across the Continent. The public anger, which included the burning of mosques in traditionally tolerant Holland, is evidence that the European instinct for survival has not yet been fully extinguished.

But that survival instinct is threatened by the multiculturalism and political correctness that has been advocated in media and academe and institutionalized in national and European Union laws and regulations for half a century. Europe's effort at cultural tolerance has slowly morphed into a surprisingly deep self-loathing of Western culture that has denied the instinct for cultural and national self-defense.

Europe's horror at what it did to itself and the world in the First and Second World Wars led to the great denationalizing effort of a European Union. In World War I, the very idea of nationalism as a virtue was drowned in a sea of blood in the trenches of France, and Hitler's repulsive cult of the superior Aryan race rendered any future claims to cultural or racial pride detestable.

As Europe lay culturally humiliated and economically bereft after World War II, the noble instinct to rebuild as a tolerant, denationalized, and economically united entity emerged. At the same time, the trend away from religious faith and toward secularism—which had started three hundred years before, in the French Enlightenment—accelerated. The horror of World War II's sixty million deaths worldwide, and its appalling culmination in the Nazi death camps, doubtless gave impetus to the average European's fading faith in God and religion.

Arising out of those ashes, Europe went about the business of rebuilding its prosperity on the basis of an ever more federated economy. As the European states began to prosper, they built an overly generous welfare and retirement system, while reducing the number of hours the average European worked.

But in one of history's cruelest jokes, these European experiences, instincts, and trends began to reach a critical mass in overextended social welfare programs, loss of religious faith, cultural passivity, and blindness to foreign dangers, just as insurgent Islam came racing toward Europe and the West.

Europe certainly had a role in developing the Islamic world as a colonizer, as a partitioner of the Middle East after World War I, as a role model for Arab socialism and fascism, and now as an investor. But the timing of the two civilizations' evolutions is largely a historic accident.

If insurgent Islam had arisen even a generation earlier, Europe would doubtlessly have put it down with her traditional confidence, acumen, and ruthlessness. If the clash were to have come another generation from now, she almost certainly would be too reduced in vigor to fend it off. But coming as it is now, it is unclear whether Europe will be able to rise and effectively defend her culture.

But I believe a case can be made, and very reasonably hoped for, that Europe's current trends of the last half-century are even now beginning to reverse. Just as America turned sharply to the right a generation ago—returning to freer markets, a religious revival, traditional values, increased birthrates, military strength, and national pride—so will Europe take a similar path in time to reinvigorate its culture and hold off, for the third time in history, an Islamic challenge to the West.

We Americans should certainly hope that Europe will revive, because it is in our deepest strategic interests that she do so. The Islamist insurgency is only in its early stages. It will grow more intense and amass a broader foundation of support around the world. We can't know its ultimate outcome, but it will surely be seen as one of history's major transformations.

If Europe doesn't rise to the Islamic challenge, Eurabia will come to pass. Then Europe will cease to be an American ally and instead become a base of operations (as she already is to a small degree) against us.

In this regard, there is a clear analogy to World War II, and we would be well advised to remember that history. From the late 1930s until December 8, 1941, most Americans thought that isolation was the wisest policy. Let Hitler take Europe; we are safe in our continental fortress. But Franklin Roosevelt believed that we would ultimately have to fight the Nazis because we could not long sustain our culture in a world dominated by Nazism. I believe he was right then, and the isolationists (or realists, as they self-approvingly call themselves today) are wrong now, because we cannot live within the constrictions of a world dominated by radical Islam.

Even if we could limit and recover from repeated radical Islamist terrorist attacks, the sense of isolation (of existential loneness) in the world would turn us ever more in on ourselves—making us more crabbed, paranoid, and spiritually deformed. It would be survival, of a sort, but it would be far different from the future we dream of for our grandchildren.

A big part of the problem in understanding the Islamist threat comes from the lack of obvious words to describe it. As linguists explain, an important role of language is its capacity to evoke cognitive images that mold our notion of reality. The right word or phrase creates an understanding and opens concepts in our minds of things we can't see.[2]

For example, without the word "love," sentences, paragraphs, sonnets, or whole volumes would be needed to create and communicate the idea. There are different kinds of love, yet the use of that one word effectively conveys a whole set of sentiments and relationships that most people immediately understand. The word is not a description, but an evocation of an idea.[3] And wrong words can create wrong mental concepts. From its inception, the phrase "War on Terror" has been a deeply flawed description, because the danger is more than terrorist attacks, and our response has to be greater than preventing terrorist attacks. We are facing a challenge of immigration, cultural aggression, and a conflict of values, religions, and lifestyles. Professor Samuel Huntington's "Clash of Civilizations" is a closer approximation of the danger, but even that is insufficient. Professor Huntington, writing in 1994, described a geographic arc of danger from the Middle East to Indonesia. But in today's

globalized and Interneted world, the forces we must confront are ubiq-
uitous: They are ahead of us, behind us, and within us.

So also is the word "war" inadequate to evoke the kind of conduct
in which we are involved. World War II is what we think of as a war:
millions of uniformed soldiers and thousands of ships, tanks, and airplanes engaged in destroying the enemy's martial assets, seizing geographic locations, and eventually marching into the enemy's capital and
killing or imprisoning the enemy's leaders.

But the word "war" is correct, if inadequate, in one crucial sense. It
aptly evokes the physical danger and the need for extraordinary action
and possible sacrifice. It is also partially correct in that this struggle will
include conventional military battles. Afghanistan and Iraq were wars as
conventionally understood. There will surely be others.

Another problem with the word "war" is its recent metaphoric
usage. Over the last twenty-five years, Americans have been called to
wars against cancer, drugs, obesity, and poverty, among other bad things
we have in our lives. So "War on Terror" becomes a clichéd metaphor
that induces cynicism.

The failure to adequately describe the challenge has thrown our legal
system into disarray. As a nation of constitutional law and precedent, we
need to know legally and constitutionally where we stand. Our
Supreme Court has upheld government intrusions on civil liberties,
including enforcement of laws on sedition, censorship, and internment
of both enemy aliens and, in the case of the Japanese, American citizens,
during times of war. But these intrusions depend on specific circumstances and on whether Congress has authorized a state of war. Chief
Justice William Rehnquist wrote in 1998:

> When the President acts pursuant to an expressed or implied
> authorization of Congress, his authority is at its maximum, for it

includes all that he possesses in his own right plus all that Congress can delegate. If his act is held unconstitutional under these circumstances, it usually means that the Federal Government as an undivided whole lacks power.[4]

Today we are engaged in a "War on Terror" without the president seeking a full state-of-war status. He has merely gained authorization to fight limited actions in Afghanistan and Iraq. If he did seek a declaration of war for the "War on Terror," against whom would it be declared? On December 8, 1941, Franklin Roosevelt declared war on the Japanese empire. On April 2, 1917, Woodrow Wilson declared war on the imperial German government. President Bush and Congress manifestly could not declare war on the two remaining pillars of the president's specified "Axis of Evil"—Iran and North Korea—because the United States is not at war with Iran and North Korea, nor does it want to be at war with them. At present, the continuing insurgency in Iraq and occupation of Afghanistan are regarded as work enough. Moreover, Iran and North Korea are not the exclusive fomenters of terror, they do not exhaust the scope of the battle we face, and the Islamist terrorists who threaten us are often rogue elements who are not controlled by the countries in which they are based.

Many, if not most, of these combatants conducting or planning terror against us are in fact private citizens in countries like Britain, France, Germany, and Holland. If the governments of these countries could catch and stop the terrorists, they would (and they are). In the parlance of military strategists, the terrorist enemy is a "non-state actor," and because there is no government against which to declare comprehensive war, the maximum authority of the federal government to prosecute the war cannot be invoked. Yet, at the same time, we are in maximum peril.

Even if Congress declared a general full state of war (and delegated the maximum authority described by Chief Justice Rehnquist to the president), one does not need to possess too lurid an imagination to conjecture that such authority might be insufficient to permit America to fight, survive, and win against the amorphous (but potentially mortal) threat currently posed by insurgent Islam. The traditional, constitutional war powers are massive and intrusive. They may well be sufficient, but they might not be enough. The challenge we face might require constitutional amendments.

So the question arises: Why has President Bush not sought full constitutional war-fighting authority from Congress? Or if he thinks he possesses such authority either inherently or by implication from the congressional war authorizations against Iraq and Afghanistan, why hasn't he exercised it? Even measured against former presidents and other world leaders, the president is bold and assertive, and those who know him best are convinced that he is fully aware of the existential threat that America faces from insurgent radical Islamists. The man is so determined to try to protect our country that he has been prepared to upset the entire international order, flout the United Nations, outrage our closest European allies, destabilize friendly Middle Eastern governments, fight two wars, and risk his presidency.

And yet he has neither sought nor exercised full war powers. I would suggest that even George the Bold has hesitated because he correctly judges that a majority of the public, the politicians, and the media do not believe we are actually in a war, and that in the absence of a word, a phrase, or a concept that convincingly describes this dangerous-as-war-but-different condition, the public can only assume that we are in a state of less than war. In fact, I believe we are in a condition of more than war.

This strange war-but-not-war situation that we find ourselves in was shrewdly described by William S. Lind, former Democratic senator Gary Hart's military adviser, and four Army and Marine Corps officers in a recent *Marine Corps Gazette* article describing what they call "fourth-generation warfare" between a nation-state and non-state actors:

> In broad terms, fourth-generation warfare seems likely to be widely dispersed and largely undefined; the distinction between war and peace will be blurred to the vanishing point. It will be nonlinear, possibly to the point of having no definable battlefields or fronts. The distinction between "civilian" and "military" may disappear. Actions will occur concurrently throughout all participants' depths, including their society as a cultural, not just a physical entity.[5]

In an odd way, we are in a situation similar to that which confronted the American Indians when European explorers landed on these shores. From North America to South America, the Indians vastly outnumbered the intruders. But the Europeans were not exactly an army, and warfare did not exactly break out. Indeed, both sides seemed almost friendly and cooperative at times. Had the Europeans been seen as a threat, the Indians could have slaughtered them in short order. Even with their guns, there were only a few hundred Europeans, while there were hundreds of thousands of Indians.

Only gradually did the intrusion—driven in part by exploration and a quest for trade—gain in magnitude, change in intent, establish beachheads, and eventually overwhelm the native population. The Indians lost, despite their vast material and numerical advantages and superior knowledge of the geography of what turned out to be a battlefield, because they had no point of reference in their history to properly judge what was happening.

Today, the challenge for America and the West is to remain alert to the fact that today's Islamist insurgency is something different from anything we have experienced before. For Europeans, it is something different from even the earlier Muslim expansions.

Because it is something new for us, our laws, traditions, ethical codes, and concepts of friend and foe have not evolved to recognize and manage the threat. As the great American jurist Oliver Wendell Holmes wrote, "The life of the law has not been logic, it has been experience." Because our law and cultural institutions have not experienced a great cultural insurgency in a globalized, Interneted, and biological, chemical, and nuclear weapon–filled world, we must consider with cool logic to what extent our self-imposed historic standards of conduct are sufficient to protect us from this new danger.

As often is the case, Abraham Lincoln said it best:

The dogmas of the quiet past are inadequate to the stormy present. The occasion is piled high with difficulty, and we must rise with the occasion. As our case is new, so we must think anew, and act anew.[6]

This book is an effort at thinking anew about providing our grandchildren with the America we want them to have.

CHAPTER THREE

The Threat

L ET ME START THIS CHAPTER WITH the rather obvious concession that I am no Islamic scholar or terrorism expert. As a former lawyer and politician, and later journalist and political commentator, it was only after the shock of September 11, 2001, that I focused my thinking and research on the newly revealed danger of radical Islamic terrorism.

When I worked in Congress in the 1990s as Speaker Newt Gingrich's press secretary and senior adviser, I learned much from Congress's anti-terrorism experts. Former congressman Bill McCollum founded the congressional task force on terrorism in the 1980s. He and his staff regularly briefed us about Islamic terrorists, and they identified Osama bin Laden very early on as a potential threat to America. But like most people in Washington who don't specialize in terrorism, I didn't pay nearly enough attention. It was just one issue among hundreds that I and most of the politicians and journalists in Washington glanced at when it might briefly come into the news or legislative cycle. Not only did we not connect the dots, most of us didn't even count up the number of dots the experts were showing us.

After September 11, I focused on trying to understand, in a practical political sense, the threat facing our nation. As someone who had spent twenty years in Washington politics and policy—first on Ronald Reagan's White House staff and later as Speaker Gingrich's top aide—I needed to understand the issue well enough to be able to make practical suggestions about what we as a country could do about it.

Genuine specialists, sub-specialists, and sub-sub-specialists are capable of understanding—at remarkable depth—a small piece of the truth about a topic. But a nation, as a whole, makes its collective life-and-death decisions—for better and worse—through politics. The politician's (and the citizen's) role is to review the expert analysis, recognizing that even the best experts and scholars are at least partly subjective and given to focusing excessively on their own pet theories. Then the politician applies the experts' knowledge, his own political knowledge, the lessons of history so far as he knows them, and his own understanding of his country to the twofold question: What is the threat, and what is to be done about it? Making such decisions is not beyond the competence of citizens and politicians, and in any event, it is the politicians' judgments, and the judgments of the citizens who elect them, that will decide the policy. Experts don't make government policy. They merely give advice and analysis. Here's my own assessment of the situation we find ourselves in.

BIN LADEN IS ONLY PART OF THE PROBLEM

Because of the shocking way in which the danger was brought to our attention on September 11, most people see bin Laden and his al Qaeda organization as the target of the War on Terror. Many of President Bush's opponents during election year 2004 not only taunted him for not yet capturing bin Laden, but also suggested that capturing the terrorist and his top aides was primarily what the War on Terror was all about.

But bin Laden and al Qaeda are merely the most visible symptoms of a far more basic discontinuity in the world condition. The theory and practice of Islam have been changing for almost a century now. That change reached a critical mass in the 1990s and exploded onto the world stage most visibly to us on September 11, 2001.

Of course, all religions are in constant flux. American evangelical Protestantism expresses itself culturally and politically far differently today than it did in the early twentieth century. Prior to the 1970s, evangelical Christians tended to keep out of politics on an organized basis because they didn't want to taint their religion with such worldly business. Then, in the 1970s, they began to engage in American politics as a defensive strategy because they felt that politics and government were intruding into their daily lives. *Roe* v. *Wade*'s legalizing of abortion was the most prominent factor in that regard. That change in view and strategy had powerful consequences for America's electoral politics—a dynamic shift that many evangelical Protestants and other Americans still don't fully comprehend. But those of us in professional politics were very interested in understanding the political and electoral implications of those changes. If we had an intrinsic interest in the theology involved, it would have been personal, not professional.

Likewise, Islam is rapidly changing today. Ordinary Muslims care about these changes for personal reasons of faith. Muslim scholars care for the sake of their scholarship and are in furious academic debate regarding all the causes and likely effects of changing Muslim beliefs and practices.

For the rest of us, these changes are of interest because they have secular consequences. This is a political, not a religious, book. For the purposes of this book, I am not interested in the religious or theological aspects of Islam, except as they have implications for world politics and events.

There has been a ferocious debate—both within Islam and among Western analysts of the Islamic terrorist threat—over whether Islam is inherently warlike or peaceful, whether it is compatible with democratic government, and so on. And, of course, both sides of that debate assert that the Koran is unambiguous on these issues.

For the purposes of this book, I am going to focus only on what today's Muslims believe their religion requires them to do, think, and say. I will remain agnostic on the "true" teachings of Islam, whatever they may be. From a policymaking view, it is what Muslims say and do now that is the measure of the political, cultural, and military danger facing the West.

Unlike most other religious developments around the world today (such as the spread of Christianity in the Southern Hemisphere) that have benign or at least nonviolent consequences, the overwhelming political fact deriving from the ferment in Islam is that, to some degree, some percentage of the world's Muslims are prepared to, and actually are, murdering large numbers of people in what they feel is their religious duty. Such Islamic violence spans the globe—from America, to Russia, to Spain, to Africa, to Southeast Asia, and of course to the Middle East.

Larger numbers of Muslims are, to some degree, supportive or protective of these killers. A yet larger number of Muslims, while not supportive of such tactics, share many of the terrorists' religious convictions and perceptions. The radical currents within Islam drive some Muslims to terrorism. It drives others to a different, and more adversarial, view of their relationship to the nations and cultures in which they find themselves, whether in Paris, London, Hamburg, Rotterdam, or elsewhere around the world, including the United States. When they challenge and threaten the cultures and laws of the non-Muslim countries in which they live, that too becomes a political fact we need to acknowledge.

Muslim populations in Europe are already beginning to affect not only European domestic policy, but foreign policy as well. Many observers suspect that France's refusal to support America in the Iraq War was driven, at least in part, by French president Jacques Chirac's need for the Muslim vote, which is now about 10 percent of the total French electorate.

Of course, just as no one at the time could anticipate the historic consequences of Paul's conversion on the road to Damascus, or Martin Luther's posting of his theses on the door of a church in Wittenberg, or the emergence of the first or second great Christian awakenings in England and America, neither can we know the full historic consequences of Islam's current storms. But one would have to be willfully obtuse not to strongly suspect that we are seeing the beginning of something likely to have profound effects on world history over the next several generations.

To point out the obvious, the resurgence of a militant Islam drove America to fight two wars in Muslim countries in two years, disrupted America's alliance with Europe, caused the largest reorganization of American government in half a century (with the creation of the Department of Homeland Security), changed election results in Europe, and threatened the stability of most of the governments in the Middle East. It drove America to pressure Saudi Arabia to change the way it teaches religion to its children and to other Muslim children (through its madrasses) around the world, and forced America to pressure Indonesia, the Philippines, Pakistan, and Somalia, among others, to change their domestic security policies. In the case of nuclear-armed Pakistan, the

United States has had to coerce the Pakistani government to change sides regarding the Taliban and to be a somewhat unwilling ally of the United States in our war against terrorism. As a result, Pakistani president Pervez Musharraf has already suffered two assassination attempts, and we risk turning the Pakistani government and its nuclear arsenal over to fundamentalists as quickly as a bullet's flight or a bomb's explosion. America has had to build a ring of bases in Central Asia across what used to be the Muslim part of the Soviet Union. And we are only four years removed from the September 11 attacks.

But all these reactions to the perceived uprising in Islam are likely to be but an overture to the rewriting of Western policy as the fuller implications of Islamic change manifest themselves in the coming decades.

ISLAMIC RELIGIOUS FERMENT

One can comprehend some measure of the rapidness of change in modern Islam by the fact that scholars are currently not able to even agree on the terms they use to describe the process. Among the terms used are fundamentalist, neo-fundamentalist, Islamist, jihadist, pietistic (or sheikist) Salafist, Wahhabist, radical, extremist, and militant—sometimes in overlapping and contradictory ways.

For instance, Olivier Roy, a leading Parisian scholar of contemporary Islam, limits the use of the term "Islamist" to Muslims who seek to apply Islam comprehensively to a state, as opposed to society in general, while many Western analysts use the term as a synonym for armed jihadist or radical.

But across the range of experts—from American conservative analysts who are deeply fearful of Islam, to top European scholars who are more sympathetic to Islam's current potential for good—there is a broad area of agreement on the current state of Islam and the West.

Most experts agree that the current ferment originated in 1928 with the founding of the Muslim Brotherhood in Egypt by Hassan al-Banna. The Muslim Brotherhood was the first modern mass movement of political Islam, designed to defeat Western imperialism and secularism. The Brotherhood called for a return to a supposedly pristine form of Islam as practiced by Muhammad and the early generations that followed him.

In time the Brotherhood gave rise to both moderate reform and violent jihad. The latter was championed by Sayyid Qutb between the 1940s and 1960s. His book *Signposts on the Road* became the seminal justification for jihad and terror as a necessary response to the predicament of Muslim conditions.

In Muslim lands in the Middle East and central Asia, Islamic theories emerged to challenge the legitimacy of local Muslim leaders who were seen as captives of the West opposed to genuine Islamic rule. Muslim governments saw these jihadists as their enemies and sometimes executed their leaders. Sayyid Qutb was executed by the Egyptian government in 1966.

Interlacing these developments, of course, has been the impact of Wahhabism, which converted the founder of the House of Saud in 1744. This austere, purist strain of Islam remained an inconsequential desert sect until the discovery of oil in Saudi Arabia. Backed by billions of petro-dollars since the 1970s, Saudi Arabia has been spreading aggressive anti-Western religious teaching throughout the Islamic world. Saudi Arabia is one of the major tributaries of the current raging Islamic river that threatens to wash over the West.

One of the key shifts in modern radical Islamist thought has been the new centrality of individual jihad. Jihad had never been one of the five pillars of Islam—the five commitments that every Muslim must make to be a good Muslim: profession of faith, prayer, fasting, almsgiving, and pilgrimage. But Sayyid Qutb, and those who have expanded upon his thoughts, such as Osama bin Laden, explicitly include jihad as a permanent and individual duty (*fard'ayn*). As Olivier Roy observes:

> This is probably the best criterion with which to draw a line between conservative neofundamentalists and radical ones: the latter are rightly called jihadists. Among the few writings of Osama bin Laden, the definition of jihad as a permanent and personal duty holds a central place. His concept of suicide attack is not found in Islam.[1]

Radical Islamists like bin Laden are not traditionalists. The idea of individual jihad—separating jihadist decisions from the Muslim community—is a radical departure, but it is important for recruiting potential terrorists. The appeal to individual jihad is ideally suited for the Internet age, and it is particularly suited to Muslims sitting alone in their apartments in Hamburg or Rotterdam or elsewhere looking for meaning in their lives.

As long as there were few Muslims in the West and few connections between Islam and Western lands, Westerners—except for a handful of scholars—could happily ignore the intricate theories of radical, reforming, fundamentalist, literalist, and purifying strains of Islam. But over the last thirty years, the Muslim population in Europe has expanded rapidly from a few hundred thousand to more than twenty million. And the coming of economic and cultural globalization—particularly the emergence of the Internet in the last decade—has dumped all this furious passion, theorizing, and action into Europe and, to a lesser but growing extent, into the United States.

Islam's internecine struggle has been more than transplanted to the West. Today, Muslims in Europe and the United States are arguing over their role in Western societies: Should they integrate, seclude themselves, or convert the West to Islam?

Islamization is predicted and analyzed by Bat Ye'or in her recent book *Eurabia: The Euro-Arab Axis*, which should be required reading for Europeans and Americans, policymakers and citizens alike.

Many Muslims living in Europe are content to be law-abiding, culturally integrated citizens. But according to almost all estimates, an increasing number feel some degree of alienation from European culture. There are two reasons for this. First, Europeans tend not to greet immigrants as hospitably as Americans do. But second, and more important, is the dynamic debate between the Muslims themselves. Many Muslims are beginning to believe that they have a religious duty *not* to integrate.

Among that group, some will be content to voluntarily secede from the local culture. Others will attempt to change European secular-Judeo-Christian culture into an Islamic culture. And yet others will cross over into violence (justified in their own minds irrespective of what scholars might say about what Islam teaches).

Part of the analytical problem here is that both the peaceful and violent separatists derive their motivations from the same growing Salafist movement—the movement that incorporates the radical, reformist, purifying branches of Islam. And both the peaceful and the violent wings of the Salafist movement insist that there can be no compromise with non-Islamic governments.

In trying to understand both the nature of the threat to us, and the range of options open to us to combat that threat, I need to pause here and note the emergence of the ambiguously motivated Islamic Party of Liberation (Hizb ut-Tahrir al-Islamiyya). It is, in the words of Olivier Roy, a former Islamist party that has turned neo-fundamentalist. In keeping with its Muslim Brotherhood past, it insists on creating a caliphate to rule over all Muslim people (the ummah) as part of a borderless Islamist state; it is organized by cells in forty countries; it is virulently anti-American and is both a conveyor belt and camouflage for terrorism; and yet it does not explicitly advocate terrorism. So what are Western governments to do with such an entity?

The best recent study of this movement is by Zeyno Baran, the director for international security and energy programs at the Nixon Center in Washington, D.C., and holder of Stanford University's Firestone Medal for her scholarship on Islam and democracy. Her study points out that the Islamic Party of Liberation shares the same political objectives as terrorist groups. It wants to replace the "Judeo-Christian dominated nation-state system" with a borderless ummah. Because it doesn't call for violence, it is more appealing to many Muslims and harder for Western governments to guard against.

"However," Baran warns, "upon closer analysis it is clear that [its] renunciation of violence is only superficial. Violence has been repudiated by [them], but other groups working towards the same goals that do use violence are never condemned by [them]. The groups never denounce terrorist attacks. In many ways it is part of an elegant division of labor. The group itself is active in the ideological preparation of the Muslims, while other organizations handle the planning and execution of terrorist attacks." In other words, while al Qaeda is one of the implementers of terrorism, the Islamic Party of Liberation does the groundwork of delivering the message and getting into the activist debate that ultimately leads to more recruits for terrorism.

How effective is this religious–political propaganda for Muslims living in Europe? Does it lead them to political extremism? Canadian Muslim journalist and author Irshad Manji was remarkably frank at an Aspen Institute conference in Berlin:

It mostly depends on how you define extremism. If you mean "literalism," then it is more than widespread, it is mainstream. If you mean the overt preaching of violence, then it percolates on the margins. The key is to recognize that because literalism is mainstream in Islam today, the thin minority of Muslims who have any intention of engaging in terror are nonetheless protected by the vast majority of moderate Muslims who don't know how to debate and dissent with that proclivity. . . .

We Muslims, even in the West, are routinely raised to believe that because the Koran comes after the Torah and the Bible (historically and chronologically), it is the final and therefore perfect manifesto of God's will. The Koran, we are taught, does not lend itself to the inconsistencies and ambiguities and outright contradictions and, God forbid, human editing like those earlier scriptures. Mainstream Muslims believe, as an article of faith, that the Koran is not like any other scripture. It is the summit of the holy books. This is a supremacy complex, which even moderate Muslims share. And this supremacy complex is dangerous because when abuse happens under the banner of Islam, most Muslims do not yet know how to debate, dissent, revise or reform. That's because we have not yet been introduced to the possibility, let alone the virtue, of asking questions about our holy book. The same cannot be said today for moderate Christians and Jews.

In that sense Islamic terrorism, both in the Netherlands and abroad, is able to thrive because it is embedded in a wider circle of fellow Muslims. This is the reality that most Western security experts have yet to grasp. . . .

[Because] most Muslims have never been given the permission to interpret the Koran freely, they feel it is not their place to denounce those who "know better." Islamist terrorists are expert in quoting the Koran for their purposes. To question them, it is widely felt, is to question the Koran itself, and that is off limits.

Manji went on to explain:

A second reason is the sheer fear of persecution from fellow Muslims, even in open societies such as Western Europe and North America. Let me illustrate. Despite the anger, venom and death threats I receive for having written a book called *The Trouble with Islam*, I'm much more surprised by the support, affection and even love I hear from fellow Muslims. But most of the Muslims who write to me in support, or who whisper "thank you" in my ear after a public event, tell me that they can't be public about the support. Nor do they feel that they can be vocal about their own struggles with the faith today. That's because they fear "persecution." I have engaged enough of the people who use this word to report that they mean more than ostracism. They mean physical reprisal against themselves and their families.[2]

Manji describes a process of a radical few intimidating a non-radical many into silence. This process is not unique to Muslim culture. A very similar process happened in Germany in the 1920s and 1930s. At that time, Germans were feeling humiliated and confused, and were impressionable to outside powers and influences. The Nazis, though a tiny minority of the population, were well organized and aggressive, and claimed to speak for an ancient and true German culture. They particularly targeted German youth.[3]

As the Nazis alienated young people from their parents, they both intellectually and physically intimidated "good" Germans first into silence, then into collaboration, and eventually into full support. It became both dangerous to one's health and "un-German" to oppose the Nazi movement. The Nazis had both the "winning" ideas and the strongest fists in 1930s Germany; they seemed to have the wind of history at their back. By inspiration and intimidation, they took over a nation adrift.[4]

Muslims today, in traditionally Muslim lands and in Europe, are similarly situated. Radical Islam, sometimes accurately called Islamo-fascism,[5] has all the "advantages" the Nazis had. The Islamo-fascists find a Muslim population adrift, confused, and humiliated by the dominance of foreign nations and cultures. They find a large youthful population increasingly disdainful of their parents' passive habits.

Just as the Nazis reached back to German mythology and the supposed Aryan origins of the German people, the radical Islamists reach back to the founding ideas and myths of their religious culture. And just like the Nazis, they claim to speak for authentic traditions while actually advancing expedient and radical innovations. The Islamo-fascist mullahs encourage young Muslims not to turn to their parents for guidance on choosing a wife (or wives); nor are they to be guided by any parental or community disapproval of making an individual commitment to jihad. They are even allowed to drink alcohol, shave their beards, and commit what would otherwise be judged immorality in a Muslim in order to advance the jihad.

In many ways, these new radical Muslim fundamentalists are post-modern, not pre-modern. They are designing a distinctly Western, fascistic version of Islam that is less and less connected to the Islam of their Middle Eastern homeland.[6] Radical Western Islam brings with it the combative strength and deep faith of its authentic traditions while constantly modifying itself to best attack liberal, secular European and American institutions.

The idea of individual jihad is a particularly critical innovation. Traditionally, only the doctors of Islamic law, the *ulema*, were authorized to declare armed jihad. According to traditional doctrine, the jihad is a force that restores harmonious order to the world, while a *fitna*—a seditious activity that threatens to fragment the faithful Muslim community—is the opposite. Only the ulema can officially distinguish between the two and, therefore, only the ulema can legally declare jihad in its extreme form of armed struggle.[7] By overturning the prerogative of the ulema, the radical neo-fundamentalists have vastly empowered themselves to organize and fight the West without the restraints of traditional Islam.

Islamo-fascism exploits young people's need to feel connected to something authentic and larger than themselves, while it freely and expediently embraces such modern activities, customs, and methods as are useful and attractive to its target audience of young Muslims. The radical Islamists are able to rationalize concessions to modernity with ancient-sounding mumbo jumbo while still sounding like authentic fundamentalists, the only true voice of Islam.

The Nazis overwhelmed German society with these methods seventy years ago. And there is building evidence that the radical Islamists are moving ever more successfully down the same path—particularly within the younger generations of Muslims in Europe and, to a lesser extent, in the United States.

New York Times foreign policy columnist Thomas Friedman, reporting from Paris in January 2005, closed a column by recounting an interview he had with two eighteen-year-old Muslim girls who had been born and raised in France: "What did I learn from them? That they got all their news from al Jazeera TV, because they did not believe French TV, that the person they admire most in the world is Osama bin Laden, because he was defending Islam, that suicide martyrdom was justified because there was no greater glory than dying in defense of Islam, that they saw themselves as Muslims first and French citizens last, and that all their friends felt pretty much the same."[8]

Many young Muslims in Europe, and some in America, particularly second- and third-generation Muslims, cannot be considered part of a Muslim diaspora. They are no longer strongly connected to their family's country of origin, nor do they intend to return. Instead, they are forming their own Muslim consciousness from the Internet, books, videotapes, and audiotapes, where radical ideas and mullahs dominate.

As French Islamic scholar Gilles Kepel describes it:

On websites in every European language, whether jihadist or pietist, trendy jargon blends in with an intense polemic founded on obscure religious references to medieval scholars. In chat rooms, linguistic shortcuts mingle with a profusion of Islamic formulas. In the midst of an English text one finds PBUH (for Praise be upon him) in Arabic script. All of this debate and intensity seems completely unrelated to the social and cultural reality of European Islam as it is lived in the workers' cities. Yet this strange language serves to express some of the tensions that pull members of these communities to one side and then the other.[9]

The Internet has many radical Islamic "experts" and mullahs who function like Dear Abby. European Muslims pose questions on everything from whether to be polite to infidels to how to prepare for jihad, and the "expert" provides an immediate answer, often a hodgepodge of Koranic citations, quotes from ancient scholars, and the expert's own advice.

It is in this constantly morphing digital environment that a new, increasingly radical Islam is emerging in Europe. Disconnected from their homelands, isolated from their non-Muslim neighbors and fellow workers, alienated from their elders, Europe's young Muslims are finding a weird, disembodied, globalized radical Islam appealing. But not just Muslims.

Converts to Islam are a growing element. Olivier Roy identifies four categories of converts: politicized rebels; religious nomads; former drug addicts and petty thieves; and blacks, Latinos, and persons of mixed race.[10] The first category is catching European youth who would have been swept up in Marxist movements a generation ago. John Walker Lindh—the California al Qaeda member caught in Afghanistan—typifies this category. Drug addicts and thieves are seeking structure and support. Some young blacks and Latinos find radical Islam a "rebuke" to a European or American society they feel has rejected them. Of course, these converts are "an intense focus of terrorist networks"[11] precisely because they do not "look" Muslim.

Prisons are obviously fertile recruiting grounds for terrorists. And because of a false sense of tolerance and an almost inexplicable ignorance, prison authorities in both America and Europe permit radical Wahhabist mullahs to work inside prisons, as though they were in the same category as Catholic priests or Methodist ministers.

A generation ago, the American Black Muslim movement, whatever else might be said about it, went into the prisons and reclaimed young criminals to a life of good manners, gainful employment, respect for women, self-respect, and lawfulness. Today, the radical Muslim recruiters are enlisting a criminal legion into the ranks of Islamic terrorists.

It is hard to quantify the current attitudes of Muslims in Europe because recent polling is spotty. But in Britain, the *Guardian* newspaper has done some reliable polling. In March 2004, 13 percent of British Muslims favored more terrorist attacks on the United States. Another *Guardian* poll from November 2004 found that 86 percent of British Muslims were against the use of violence in Britain to gain political objectives. This was cited as good news by the liberal newspaper. However, it is appalling that more than one in ten British Muslims would admit to a pollster that they were in favor of political terrorism in the country they called home.

In November 2004, 61 percent of British Muslims wanted sharia law, rather than British law, applied to Muslims in Britain for civil matters, assuming it did not violate regular British law. And in the same sample, one in four British Muslims (26 percent) believed that the Muslim community has already integrated too much into British society. That is up from 17 percent in a previous poll. Thirty-three percent think more integration should occur, but that number is down sharply from 41 percent in a previous poll.

Although those absolute numbers are fairly disturbing, their rapid movement should be even more alarming. A drop in support for integration into society from over four in ten to barely three in ten is an unambiguous indicator that the radical, culturally assertive argument is quickly winning the day in the already established British Muslim community. New immigrants are overwhelmingly likely to be even more hostile to Western culture.

While there are few good numbers available to objectively measure the magnitude of this aggressive cultural attitude, some numbers and events are suggestive of the growing danger.

In June 2004, Ken Macdonald, British director of public prosecutions, reported that he might reopen the criminal investigations of 117 British Muslim women who had been suspected victims of "honor killings." Muslim men, under Muslim traditional laws, are allowed to kill their wives, daughters, and sisters if they are "perceived to bring dishonor on their families."[12]

In January 2005, the London *Times* reported that British Muslim cleric Omar Bakri Muhammad was using his Internet site to condone suicide terrorist attacks and urge young British Muslims to join al Qaeda. "I believe the whole of Britain has become Dar al-Harb [land of war]. In such a state the kuffar [non-believer] has no sanctity for their own life or property," he said. He went on to advise one Muslim woman that she was permitted to become a suicide bomber.

Bakri told the London *Times* that he was not calling for violent action in the UK, and claimed that his definition of Britain as Dar al-Harb was "theoretical."[13] A few days later, he wrote, "Al-Qaeda and all its branches and organizations of the world, that is the victorious group and they have the emir and you are obliged to join. There is no need to mess about."

Two nights later he asserted that the voices of dead mujahideen were calling on young Muslim Britons to fight. "These people are calling you and shouting to you from far distant places: al jihad, al jihad. They say to you, my dear Muslim brothers, 'Where is your weapon, where is your weapon? Come on to the jihad.'"

While the British authorities could detain Bakri if he were deemed a terrorist associate, under the Anti-terrorism Crime and Security Act, they had not yet done so, even after these broadcasts.[14]

On a slightly different front, the British Advertising Standards Authority reported in January 2005 that British Muslims have stepped

up a campaign of defacing or tearing down public billboards that fea-
ture ads that elements in the Muslim community consider inappropri-
ate, such as ads for perfume, hair dye, undergarments, and certain
television shows.[15]

In April 2004, Germany's Office for the Protection of the Constitution (one of three German intelligence services) issued a major report
on Islamic extremism in Germany. While the report identified 57,300
specific Muslims as "radical" (German bureaucrats are justly renowned
for their careful attention to detail, supported by impeccable record
keeping), Otto Schilly, the German interior minister, stated that the
extremist Islamist groups commanded a much larger number of covert
sympathizers and had extended their influence to a wider swath of the
Muslim population than in the previous year. He added that these
groups are reaching many more people with their "disintegrative activities" that were "in particular attracting a younger following."

Schilly expressed concern that the largest Islamic organization in Germany, Milli Gorus, while still technically a legal operation under German
law, had developed "a strong anti-Western and anti-democratic character." The organization specifically tries to indoctrinate Muslims living in
Germany. "We're very critical of their youth work," said Schilly.[16]

In November 2004, German television broadcast the words and
images of a Turkish imam in Germany urging his Bavarian congrega-
tion to "take advantage of democracy to further our cause."[17]

In December 2004, Norwegian prime minister Kjell Magne Bondevik expressed disappointment that "most of Norway's top politicians,
but very few imams, participated in a torchlight protest march against
violence and terrorism" that had been organized to express outrage at
Theo van Gogh's murder in nearby Holland. The march came just days
after Zahid Mukhtar, the spokesman for the Islamic Council in Norway,

had said, on national television, that he could "understand that Muslims had been provoked by van Gogh's latest film, and that he could understand why someone murdered him." Most Muslim leaders in Norway boycotted the protest march.[18]

Meanwhile, in Canada, the debate about whether to establish sharia law for Canadian Muslims is heating up. In 2004, former Ontario attorney general Marion Boyd suggested the possibility of applying sharia under a 1991 Canadian arbitration law.

Farzana Hassan-Shahid, the president of Muslims Against Terrorism, Canada, says that Canadian Muslims are debating what is "now being perceived as a battle between devout Muslims, and those who are Muslim in name only, whose sole objective is to denigrate Islam and vilify Muslims."[19] This argument, that if you are not radical, you are not a good Muslim, is of a piece with the Nazi argument of the 1920s and 1930s—if you were not a Nazi, you were not a good German and not a good child of the fatherland.

It is a radical Islamist manipulation of Islamic tradition to argue that sharia should apply in the West. Sharia was meant to apply in Muslim lands, which Europe and North America are not. Non-Islamic lands were designated either Dar al-Harb, the land of war, or Dar al-Sulh, the land of truce. Traditional, non-jihadist Muslims designate Europe the land of truce, where neither sharia nor jihad would be legitimate. But radical groups like the European Fatwa Council, which is the legal arm of the British-based Federation of Islamic Organisations in Europe (FIOE), have redesignated Europe as part of "the land of Islam." Thus, they assert that Muslims are entitled to be judged by sharia law, rather than the enacted law of the European country where they live.[20] It is almost inevitable that the side calling for the return to an allegedly more devout, more authentic Islam is going to win these battles within the Muslim communities.

Once a Muslim in the West has accepted this first premise of returning to "devout" Islam, as opposed to "Islam in name only," it becomes progressively harder to oppose the terrorist elements within the community. For example, in the same November 2004 *Guardian* newspaper poll in Britain (which found that 86 percent of Muslims were opposed to the use of violence to gain their political ends), only about 70 percent told pollsters they would turn in a fellow Muslim if he were a terrorist.

So by the end of 2004, about one in ten British Muslims admit to being willing to commit terrorist acts, and one in three admit to being willing to protect Muslim terrorists from lawful authorities, while six in ten want to be governed by Muslim sharia law rather than by British law. Virtually every law enforcement organization, intelligence expert, and Islamic scholar believes the trend continues to move strongly toward such attitudes and away from traditional, law-abiding, assimilating intentions.

Muslim parts of Paris, Rotterdam, and other European cities are already labeled "no-go zones" for ethnic Europeans, including armed policemen. As the Muslim populations—and their level of cultural and religious assertiveness—expand, European geography will be "reclaimed" for Islam. Europe will become pockmarked with increasing numbers of "little Fallujahs" that will be effectively impenetrable by anything much short of a U.S. Marine division.

Thus, as the ersatz, Westernized, Internet-communicated fundamentalism expands its reach into European (and, perhaps, to a lesser extent, American) Muslim communities, not only will Islamic cultural aggression against a seemingly passive and apologetic indigenous population increase, but the zone of safety and support for the actual terrorists will expand as well. These conditions pose three related but distinct threats to Europe and the West:

1. The cultural dominance of Europe by Islam
2. The price of European resistance to such dominance if the Europeans do resist
3. The increased danger of actual terrorist attacks that can be planned and launched from Islamists securely based in Europe

I've already described the first threat. Let me now briefly discuss the second threat. If the current leaders of Europe do not respond to the Islamist threat boldly and effectively, the common European people might decide to defend their culture as vigilantes. In that case, Europe will again become a bloody urban battleground. This would be a temporary tragedy for liberal principles of governance, but would at least secure Europe from Muslim domination over the next half-century.

The harm, however, of a vigilante people's effort against the radical Islamists can be mitigated, if not avoided, if the governments themselves will lead the struggle for European cultural survival. It should be a prime objective of American policy to encourage the European governments and the European Union to lead their people in this struggle, rather than follow them.

Keep in mind that Europe is only too familiar with organized mass violence—both directed by governments and arising from the people. From eighteenth-century revolutionary France, through the revolutionary and counter-revolutionary street violence of the nineteenth century, to the streets of Berlin and elsewhere in the interwar years of 1919 to 1933, to the Balkan atrocities and wars of the 1990s, European people have often fought before yielding to unacceptable conditions.

Remember, too, European people have willingly participated in the massive Napoleonic wars and two world wars—all powerful evidence of an inherent European trait to fight rather than succumb. And it is noteworthy that in November 2004, after van Gogh's murder, the usually peaceful and tolerant Dutch people firebombed more than a dozen Muslim schools and cultural centers.

Though it seems inconceivable that peaceable, no longer nationalistic, social welfare–drugged post–World War II Europe could again turn to mass violence and bloodshed, many once thought it was also inconceivable that Europe could suffer two world wars in the twentieth century. Before World War I, Europeans thought they had left their bloody past behind them, having substituted for it economic prosperity, international trade, and cousin kings on the thrones of the three great monarchist powers of Britain, Germany, and Russia. Moreover, Europe hadn't had a continental war in almost a hundred years, not since the Napoleonic Wars that ended in 1815.

It was often observed in the first decade of the twentieth century that Europe could not afford to go to war with itself again because of the prosperity coming from trade and commerce. It was also observed that, should problems arise, surely the cousin kings would never fight each other. And yet, without notice, Europe slipped into the Great War in August 1914.

Again, after World War I, Europeans were convinced that maintaining the European peace was absolutely necessary. There could be no repetition of the horrors of World War I. And yet World War II followed—and not only did vast national armies fight to the death without significant mutinies, but populations under Nazi domination had heroic resistance movements from Norway to Holland to France to Yugoslavia to Greece, and even, to a limited extent, in Germany.

If one had asked common European people in 1938 (as I did in the 1960s when, as a student tourist, I talked with former World War II resistance fighters) whether they could have imagined carrying rifles, blowing up German tanks, and risking death, they would have said (and did say afterward) that it was inconceivable.

They never imagined war was possible again. They were students, shopkeepers, teachers, doctors—quiet, peace-loving, middle-class folk.

Now, sixty years after the last world war, Europeans again can't imagine ever reverting to the old, bloody, heroic ways. For sixty years they have been denationalizing their psyches and ever more closely federating their economic activity, and they are now on the brink of a continental constitution (at least temporarily stalled by the French and Dutch rejection at the polls) that would return Europe to a unified condition not seen since the great division caused by the Protestant Reformation half a millennium ago. But they never planned for or dreamed of such a formidable Islamic challenge. When the first stream of Muslims came to Europe in the 1960s, they were just "guest workers" happy to have even menial jobs. Only in 2005 are the people and governments of Europe beginning to think seriously about the implications of the Islamic threat.

This time there will be no need for Europeans to resort to blood violence to defend their culture, if their governments will lead the way. Laws, including sedition laws exclusively targeted against radical Islamists, will have to be enacted to protect European culture from Islamic subversion. Some liberal principles of equal protection under the law and the right of free speech will have to be curtailed as they apply to the Islamist threat. But if European governments will not lead and enact laws of cultural self-protection, the common people will see violence and vigilantism as the only way to defend their historic culture and ways.

Of course, only time will tell whether Europeans will resist or acquiesce in this clash of civilizations. If the governments resist, the West will be strengthened. If the European governments acquiesce, but their people resist, then the resistance will be bloody and liberal principles will be traduced more than they than need to be. But if the Europeans acquiesce altogether, they will lose their culture—and Eurabia will turn what had been a continent of American allies into a continent that threatens the United States.

The third threat, which most directly and immediately challenges the United States, is that Europe has already become the most dangerous base from which terrorist attacks against us can be planned and launched. Every day that European governments do not begin to turn the tide against radical and jihadist Islamism on their continent is a day of increased mortal danger for the United States.

FUTURE TERRORISM

What sort of physical, cultural, and economic destruction might future Islamist terrorist attacks inflict on the West?[21] It is hard to find an expert who doubts that Islamist terrorism is and will continue to be a mortal threat for the foreseeable future. Even terrorism experts who are President Bush's harshest critics share that conviction, although you would never know it from the media coverage.

In presidential election year 2004, the two most highly publicized "anti-Bush" books by terror experts were *Against All Enemies*, by Richard Clarke, and *Imperial Hubris*, by Michael Scheuer. Clarke was the White House's top anti-terrorism aide in the Clinton years and during part of the Bush administration, while Scheuer led the Osama bin Laden unit at the CIA until late 2004. Clarke garnered vast publicity by accusing the Bush administration of missing the warning signs before the September 11 terrorist attacks. But much of his book, as well as his other public utterances, focused on how great the terrorist threat still is.

Likewise, Scheuer's book took President Bush to task for mismanaging the War on Terror, but also focused on the magnitude of the terrorist threat. He wrote, "Americans, particularly the elites, refuse to grasp...that their country is engaged in war to the death with an enemy who has warned us of his every move and intention. Whatever comes next, whatever disaster befalls us, our children, and our country, we were warned and chose not to fight to our utmost."[22]

He went on to explain that the terrorist threat is so great that unless we try to satisfy bin Laden and his organization by acceding to all their demands, we will be forced to fight with all our military strength:

> And it is not the option of daintily applying military power as we have since 1991. "U.S. soldiers are unprepared for the absolute mercilessness of which modern warriors are capable," Ralph Peters correctly said in *Fighting for the Future: Will America Triumph?*, "and they are discouraged or prohibited by their civilian masters and their own customs from taking the kind of measures that might be effective against members of the warrior class." To secure as much of our way of life as possible, we will have to use military force in the way Americans used it on the fields of Virginia and Georgia, in France and on the Pacific islands, and from skies over Tokyo and Dresden. Progress will be measured by the pace of killing, and yes, by body counts. Not the fatuous body counts of Vietnam, but precise counts that will run to extremely large num-

bers. The piles of dead will include as many or more civilians as combatants because our enemies wear no uniforms.[23]

When I interviewed Scheuer for this book, he agreed with me that the media—both in the United States and in Europe—had ignored his warning about the severity of the Islamist terrorist threat. The media chose to focus instead on his harsh criticism of President Bush's foreign policy.

In fact, Scheuer argues (and I strongly disagree) that the best way for America to avoid terrorism's lethal blows is to comply with bin Laden's demands that we stop supporting Israel and that we keep out of the Middle East pretty much altogether. It is President Bush's support—and every previous president's support since Truman—for Israel and America's presence in the oil-rich Middle East that Scheuer refers to as *Imperial Hubris*. The alternative to such withdrawal, he believes, is total war.

This brings me to one of the primary reasons I decided to write this book. It is to give what publicity I can to the following political fact: The danger of America being horribly hit by terrorist attacks, great as it inherently is (given the capacities of the enemy), is compounded by the plain fact that the public—and much of the government and media—do not take terrorist threats seriously enough.

Since September 11, 2001, I have observed the disquieting phenomenon that the more individuals know about the threat, the more alarmed they are. One cannot find an anti-terrorism or intelligence expert who is not worried sick about the likelihood of danger. But politicians, journalists, and members of the public who have not looked closely at the matter are usually much less concerned.

Even when the top experts speak out, their statements seem to pass with little comment and even less concern. For example, in February

2005, Ronald Noble, the head of Interpol (the top coordinating office for all European law enforcement agencies), announced, according to Reuters news service, that "the threat of a biological terrorist strike by al Qaeda is very real, but the world is still not prepared." Noble went on to explain:

> The number of terrorist attacks that have occurred around the world and the evidence that has been seized revealing the kind of planning that al Qaeda has done in the area of biological weapons or chemical weapons is enough evidence for me to be concerned about it. Anyone who is honest about this has to admit that if al Qaeda launches a spectacular biological attack which could cause contagious disease to be spread, no entity in the world is prepared for it. Not the U.S., not Europe, not Asia, not Africa.[24]

His statement was made only a week after the congressional testimony of CIA director Porter Goss that al Qaeda and other militants were seeking chemical, biological, or nuclear weapons, and that it "may only be a matter of time" before they use such arms.[25]

A week later, Sir Ian Blair, chief of the Metropolitan Police in London, warned that there was an ongoing terror threat in Britain from "very many" Muslim men, and that the danger was so great that it justified stopping and searching Muslim-looking men in London even if the police had no suspicion of illegal conduct.[26]

Keep in mind that law enforcement and intelligence services are predisposed to understate dangers when making public comment, for fear of creating a panic. But now, far from inducing panic, public warnings issued by the most senior officials of the top security agencies in the West, describing catastrophic harm from Islamist terrorist attacks, induce only inattention and indifference. As a result, even the most modest protective half-measures by Western governments are ferociously blocked by a combination of local Muslim organizations, civil-liberties activists, and political opponents. And yet we know that there are al Qaeda, Hezbollah, and other terrorist cells in the United States and Europe that are ready, willing, and probably able to carry out terrorist missions.[27]

American and European borders are porous. Law enforcement agencies admit that they cannot stop terrorists from entering the country. In fact, when I interviewed Asa Hutchinson last winter, while he was still the undersecretary of Homeland Security for Border and Transportation Security,[28] he said that it was "not realistic" to think that law enforcement authorities can arrest or deport the millions of illegal aliens we know are in the country, and that taxpayers "might be afraid" to learn how much it would take in manpower and resources to control the nation's borders. He went on to say that it is "probably accurate" that law enforcement officials are not even looking for the vast majority of the eight to twelve million illegal aliens thought to be in the country.

The Beltway snipers of 2002—just a man, a boy, a gun, and a car— terrified the Washington, D.C., area for weeks before they were captured. The daily occurrences in postwar Iraq are evidence of what damage and death mere conventional explosives can inflict. Most experts believe that bin Laden's peculiar predilection for seeking ever more dramatic and symbolic acts of terrorism is the reason such conventional attacks have not yet occurred in the United States. Thus, so the theory goes, he won't strike in America again until he can be more destructive than he was on September 11, 2001. When he leaves the scene, or if some other jihadist feels the call, we will be almost completely open to random acts of violence by bomb or gunfire.

Vastly more destructive (and widely deemed feasible by experts) is an attack by a radiological device—a "dirty bomb" of conventional explosives packaged with radiological material. According to a recent assessment by the prestigious Council on Foreign Relations (considered to reflect the judgment of the U.S. foreign policy establishment, not a hot-headed organization), a dirty bomb takes little more expertise to set off than a conventional explosive. The only challenge lies in obtaining radiological material. The Council reported that it believes that al Qaeda acquired such material in 2002, and that documents seized in Herat, Afghanistan, in 2003 disclosed that al Qaeda had built such a device. Such radiological material is available all around the world in universities, hospitals, and other low-security locations. Higher-grade material is believed to have been stolen from various locations in the former Soviet Union.[29]

While a dirty bomb would not kill more people than a conventional explosive, a contaminated area might be uninhabitable for weeks, months, years, or even decades, depending on the grade of radiological material used in such an explosion.[30] If such a device with relatively high-grade radiological material went off in a major city, the economic effect could be appalling, leaving a downtown area uninhabitable for years. Probably more economically damaging than the loss of specific businesses would be the crash in real estate values in urban areas. Millions of both residential and commercial property owners would probably be wiped out. All of that could flow from an explosion that killed perhaps no more than dozens or hundreds of people.

According to the most prudent and cautious experts, the means to inflict this damage are available and probably already possessed by terrorists. All that stands between us and such an attack is intent and the random chance that the terrorists might be caught by law enforcement before they can act.

A biological attack could cause death and economic ruin at a level several magnitudes higher than a radiological device, depending on the germ used. The smallpox virus is highly contagious and has a mortality rate of about 30 percent. In July 2001, the United States government ran a test of emergency services reactions to a smallpox attack, which they named "Dark Winter." It simulated smallpox attacks in Oklahoma, Georgia, and Pennsylvania. "Participants discovered that despite their quickest actions, the attacks quickly spread out of control. It led to a nationwide catastrophe, a collapse of the public health system and chain reaction breakdowns of civil law and order."[31]

As Tara O'Toole of the Johns Hopkins University Center for Civilian Biodefense Strategies explained:

> There's no question when a nuclear attack has occurred, and then you're in the aftermath. You're in consequence management immediately. A biological weapons attack—as we saw, actually, in the anthrax mailings—evolves and unfolds over time. The first people who come to notice, because they're sick, are probably not the first people to get sick. Nor will they be the last to be afflicted. And it's going to be very difficult to tell early on how big the attack is. It might be very difficult to tell who's affected, who's exposed, who's at risk, whether it's one attack or multiple attacks.
>
> It might be very difficult to diagnose exactly what the weapon is. It's conceivable that someone will engineer weapons that evade normal diagnostic techniques, for example, or attack organs that aren't usually thought to be involved in one disease or another.

So, there'll be a lot more mystery and confusion in a biological weapons attack.[32]

As you read this clinical description of management challenges in the case of a biological terror attack—the reality of which would be confusion, mass death, uncontainable fear, vigilante self-defense, a transportation shutdown, economic crisis, food shortages, and heartbreak at the death of children, husbands, and wives in vast numbers—recall that the head of Interpol said "the threat of a biological terrorist strike by al Qaeda is very real, but the world is still not prepared."

The last and most instantaneously lethal form of terrorist attack is, of course, by nuclear explosion. But at this point, according to the experts, it is only conjectural whether terrorists may come to possess such a device. Its effects are obvious; its likelihood is unknown.

However, in a report issued in June 2005 by the Senate Foreign Relations Committee, which surveyed the best judgment of eighty experts worldwide on weapons of mass destruction (WMD), the grim conclusion was that there is a 70 percent chance of a successful WMD attack of some sort within the next ten years. The most likely device was judged to be a radioactive dirty bomb, followed by a biological or chemical attack, with a nuclear explosion least likely. As Senate Foreign Relations Committee chairman Senator Richard Lugar concluded, "Even if we succeed spectacularly at building democracy around the world, bringing stability to failed states and spreading economic opportunity broadly, we will not be secure from the actions of small, disaffected groups that acquire weapons of mass destruction. Everything is at risk if we fail in this one area."[33]

But what are we to make of a circumstance in which the top law enforcement and intelligence officials predict that terrorists are able and likely to carry out a dirty bomb or a biological attack—and yet the major news during such announcements is the Michael Jackson trial or Martha Stewart's release from prison? Ah well, regular, everyday life must go on—until it doesn't.

CHAPTER FOUR

Europe Reacts

FOR AMERICANS, THE WORLD CHANGED at almost exactly 9 a.m. Eastern Daylight Time, September 11, 2001. Virtually the entire nation went from indifference or ignorance of the Islamist terrorist threat to consuming fear, just as sixty years before, on December 7, 1941, Americans had shifted within minutes from complacent isolationism to joining a world at war. We tend to sleep through history until we are awoken with a start; then we grab for our guns and all hell breaks loose. We are like a deep-sleeping dog that, when kicked, wakes up barking and biting. Europeans, more catlike, doze with one eye half-open.

Unlike America, Europe has long experience with terrorism on its soil: from Basque terrorists in Spain, to homegrown leftist terrorists in Germany and Italy, to Indonesian terrorists in Holland, to Irish terrorists in Britain, to France's troubles with Muslim terrorists from Algeria. Europeans manage terrorism with intense law enforcement augmented by occasional covert or paramilitary operations and fairly intrusive intelligence efforts.

For America, September 11 was a wake-up call. Within hours, the attorney general of the United States started rounding up thousands of young Muslim men within our borders. The legal authority was tenuous, but Americans expected action—and plenty of it.

For Europeans, it was terrorist business as usual. But it also has to be said that even many of our European friends—though they wouldn't have wished the horrors of September 11 on us—thought we had it coming. In their eyes we were like the drunk who finally gets arrested for drunk driving.

To many Europeans, America was at fault for stubbornly, generously, and unquestioningly backing Israel against the "legitimate" demands of the Palestinian Arabs. We had done nothing to lower our dependence on Middle Eastern oil and had therefore been far too conspicuously backing unpopular Arab potentates. We had refused to participate in various European-led international projects such as the effort to reduce global warming and the International Criminal Court.

France in particular (but not alone in Europe) had taken to diplomatically allying itself with Arab and Muslim anti-American sentiments for reasons of profit and realpolitik against the United States. Suave, aging France was psychologically gratified to be playing the role of protective uncle to its wild, uneducated, yet deserving little Arab brothers (who doubtless would heed France's advice, sell France oil, and add street muscle to French diplomatic efforts). Like Dr. Frankenstein, France was supremely confident it could manage its newly acquired ward in the same way that it had kept Germany in its post–World War II deferential diplomatic posture.

Europe feels a natural sense of superiority over bigger, stronger, richer America. Europe considers itself the center of the world and the natural manager of it. America might come in handy from time to time—despite our oafish, ham-fisted, semi-literate ways—but such emergencies aside, Europe is certain of its cultural preeminence.

And, of course, America's impulsive—in the European view—plunge into Iraq only confirmed to Europeans that we had no idea how to handle the terrorist danger. As Charles-Maurice de Talleyrand, the eighteenth-century archetypical French statesmen, said of French revolutionary violence, "What principles can men learn from impulsive acts, the spontaneous products of unleashed passions?"

It is difficult to overstate the distorting effect the Iraq War had on European judgment from the summer of 2002 until at least the Iraqi elections of 2005. It confirmed most Europeans' opinions that whatever America said or did regarding terrorism was wrong, both substantively and ethically.

European thinking is overlaid with a far more deeply developed view of Muslims in Europe—one that goes to the heart of Europe's view of its future. Europe's elite accepted the idea that growing numbers of Muslims in Europe would be the solution to Europe's declining birthrate. European governments accepted the multicultural belief that Muslims would mesh smoothly with the legal, economic, and cultural unification of Europe through a constitutionally defined, sovereign European Union.

If the attacks of September 11 were more than the violence of a relatively small band of cutthroats, and if the attacks emerged out of general Islamic unrest in both the Middle East and the West, then the central premise of Europe's view of its future would be in serious doubt.

If the large and growing European Muslim population—not American foolishness—was the source of the current (and of future) violence, what was Europe to think? Fifty years of European planning and action, the European Union's possible expansion into Muslim Turkey, and the imminent enactment of the EU constitution would be in doubt. How could Europe accept that possibility? Not only had Jacques Chirac of France and Gerhard Schröder of Germany dedicated the remainder of their seemingly formidable careers to this goal, but the life's work of thousands of EU bureaucrats, of the governments of all the European nations, and of countless European academic and media elites, all dedicated to the creation of a secular, peaceful, prosperous European Union, would be in ashes.

The linchpin of this entire gorgeous edifice—now already two-thirds constructed—was an ever-growing, assimilated, law-abiding Muslim European population. Only a steady tide of high-birthrate Muslims could fill the ever-expanding population gap caused by the dearth of indigenous European babies. Only with these young, increasingly productive Muslim workers could Europe afford the social welfare system it had given itself. Only with these able and law-abiding workers could Europe economically compete with America and Asia in the twenty-first century and beyond.

It is thus not surprising that Europe as a whole—but particularly its leadership class—has been in the deepest possible denial of the nature of the radical Islamist threat. Of course, in the mean streets of Rotterdam, Paris, Hamburg, and London, everyday men and women found many of the local Muslim immigrants and their children brushing harshly up against them. Not only were they different, but some of them were also far from apologetic about their differences. Slowly, political opposition began to form against the Muslim immigrants, but it was seen as merely lower-class, racist elements being appropriated by upper-class remnants or the ideological heirs of Europe's prewar fascists or populist political rabble-rousers: Enoch Powell in Britain, Jean-Marie Le Pen in France, Pim Fortuyn in Holland, Jörg Haider in Austria, and lesser such lights. And of course there were also the contemptible, racist, nationalistic soccer hooligans—the yobs, the cultural lumpenproletariat, whose existence was not seen as a cultural warning but rather as a reason to redouble the multicultural project. Europeans were accustomed to about 10 percent of their populations being politically beyond the pale on both the Communist left and the racist, fascist, or monarchist right. But the events of 2004 changed the calculations.

First in Madrid, in March; then in Beslan, Russia, in September; and finally, and most stunningly, in Amsterdam, in November, Islamist terrorists struck and killed Europeans on their home soil. Although hundreds of children were killed in Russia and hundreds of commuters were slaughtered on Madrid's trains, it was the killing of a single man in Amsterdam that caused the mainline media and top European leaders to break from their previously sedate comments about Islamic terrorism and immigration.

On the morning of November 2, 2004, on a street in east Amsterdam, Theo van Gogh was bicycling to work Van Gogh, a descendant of the great Dutch painter Vincent van Gogh, had received death threats after the broadcast of his film about Islamic violence against women, which he had made with Ayaan Hirsi Ali, a liberal, female, Dutch Muslim politician who had fled Somalia after an arranged and abusive marriage.

The alleged assassin, a Dutch Moroccan Muslim and self-described jihadist named Mohammed Bouyeri, shot van Gogh off his bicycle. As van Gogh lay in the street, he pleaded, "We can still talk about it. Don't do it. Don't do it." Bouyeri responded by shooting him again, after which he slit van Gogh's throat and stabbed a knife into his chest—with a letter attached. Witnesses were quoted in the Dutch press as saying, "He was slaughtered like an animal. Cut like a tire."[1] The five-page letter, written in a mixture of Dutch and Arabic, made further threats, against Ayaan Hirsi Ali, but also against America, Holland, and Europe as a whole: "I surely know that you, O America, will be destroyed. I surely know that you, O Europe, will be destroyed. I surely know that you, O Holland, will be destroyed."[2]

In the weeks following the van Gogh assassination, public outrage lighted a major media debate on the danger of Islamist terrorism in Europe and on what Muslims in Europe were thinking and saying about their European hosts. Anti-Islamist fear and anger began to break through the surface calm perpetuated by the European elite, who had always denied, appeased, or proposed half-measures rather than truly confront the danger of radical Islam. The assassination and mutilation of van Gogh—and the retaliatory firebombings of mosques by ethnic Dutchmen—finally forced news outlets and even European leaders to face up to the full implications of September 11, 2001, and the meaning of the migration of Muslims in large and hostile numbers into the heart of Europe.

From Holland's leading tabloid newspaper, *De Telegraaf*, and Germany's liberal *Berliner Zeitung* and *Der Spiegel* (roughly, the European equivalents of the *New York Times* and *Time* magazine) came the same heated prose that could be found in the United States in the aftermath of September 11. And here in the United States, even the liberal National Public Radio Network's (NPR) "All Things Considered" reported European public fury as breathlessly as the latest developments in Brazilian rainforest depletion.

Der Spiegel wrote, "The veil of multiculturalism has been lifted, revealing parallel societies where the law of the state does not apply." The *Berliner Zeitung* headlined its story, "Fear is spreading." In Holland, the *Telegraaf* wrote, "Magazines and papers which include incitements should be suppressed, unsuitable mosques should be shut down and imams who encourage illegal acts should be thrown out of the country."

NPR's "All Things Considered" reported on what German television's ZDF TV heard after secretly placing a camera inside a mosque in Germany. The imam said (in translation): "Those Germans, those atheists, they don't shave their armpits. Their sweat spreads evil smells. They stink. They are atheists. What good do they do to us? And since they are unbelievers, in the afterlife, they can only burn in hell."

As NPR reported, the German public heard more than that. A teacher at the Riksdorfer Elementary School—a German government school that, by German court ruling three years ago, must teach its mostly Muslim students a Muslim curriculum—read an anonymous letter he received: "Germany is an Islamic country. Islam is in the home, in schools. Germans will be outnumbered. We [Muslims] will say what we want. We'll live how we want. It's outrageous that Germans demand we speak their language. Our children will have our language, our laws, our culture."

Germans were also shocked to see young local Muslims approving of van Gogh's murder, saying, "If you insult Islam, you have to pay."[3] Such inflammatory events as these led *Der Spiegel* to proclaim in November 2004 that "a debate on the integration of Muslims is raging in Germany." The article went on to report that "Computer keyboards across the country are smoking as editorialists pontificate on the pros and cons of multiculturalism. . . . It is heated and on the verge of becoming poisoned."

Heating the German national broth further is the reemergence of a call for German *Leitkultur*, the term for a dominant and guiding culture. *Der Speigel* quoted Christian Democratic Union leader Jörg Schönbohm as saying, "In the Middle Ages, ghettos were founded to marginalize the Jews. Today, some of the foreigners who live with us in Germany have founded their own ghettos because they scorn us Germans. Those who come here have to adopt the German Leitkultur.

Our history has developed over a thousand years. We cannot allow that this basis of our commonality be destroyed by foreigners."

Edmund Stoiber, the recent Bavarian Christian Social Union's candidate for chancellor, said, "We have to defend the Christian tradition of our country." Even the Social Democrat chancellor of Germany, Gerhard Schröder, called for banning head scarves for schoolteachers in German public schools. But Bassam Tibi, a moderate Muslim leader in Germany, pronounced, "Either Islam gets Europeanized or Europe gets Islamicized."

Meanwhile, the green/animal rights left of the European spectrum has started demonstrating against the Islamic Eid al-Adha, or Feast of Sacrifice, because it requires the throat-slitting of rams and lambs. In 2004, Italian police in the town of Luino had to break up left-wing demonstrators confronting angry Muslim celebrants who were chanting "Allahu Akbar" (Allah is great) in front of the Luino slaughterhouse.

In the Netherlands itself, a speaker in the Dutch Parliament, Jozias van Aartsen, noted that "jihad has come to the Netherlands"; at a memorial to van Gogh, a Dutch schoolteacher said, "This is not just a small event. It's part of the World Trade Center and Madrid. We must see this."

After van Gogh's assassination, an Islamic elementary school in the Dutch town of Uden was burned to the ground. In Eindhoven, a town about seventy-five miles south of Amsterdam, the Tariq ibn Ziyad Islamic center was bombed. In total, at least fourteen Muslim buildings and schools were attacked in the days after the killing.

A month later, a Dutch television contest asked the public to name "the greatest Dutchman ever." The most popular answer was Pim Fortuyn, a gay, anti-Muslim, anti-immigrant politician murdered in 2002 by an animal rights activist.

While major national politicians were forced to finally start talking about the conflicts between indigenous Europeans and immigrant Muslims, at the local level nasty fights have been going on for years. In Rotterdam—a longtime Socialist Party bastion—local officials were defeated in recent elections by the right-wing party Leefbaar Rotterdam (Livable Rotterdam), led by Ronald Sorensen. One of the reasons Sorensen's party is in power is that the previous administration approved the construction of the huge mosque adjacent to the Feyenoord soccer stadium. Once the mosque is complete, it will be one of the largest in Western Europe, with room for 1,500 worshippers.

"It's an insult to put it here," Sorensen was quoted in the media complaining. "Feyenoord is like Yankee Stadium. It's the temple to Dutch soccer. It's the symbol of the Dutch working class." After Sorensen and his party came into power on the anti-immigrant wave, they asked the Muslims to build their mosque someplace else. "We said we'll find another spot for you. They said no. We asked them to lower the heights of the minarets. They said no. It's a symbol of their feelings toward us. They think we are inferior because we are not Muslims."[4]

The anger spread across Holland, and there is clear evidence that it shot up after the van Gogh assassination. In 2003, a conservative Dutch politician, Geert Wilders, made the commonplace observation in public that Yasser Arafat was a "terrorist leader." This drew an Internet death threat and the subsequent arrest and conviction of a Dutch Muslim identified as "Farid A." He had warned, "Wilders must be punished with death for his fascistic comments about Islam, Muslims, and the Palestinian cause."

Wilders then split with his party, the People's Party for Freedom and Democracy, and formed his own party around the issues of anti-immigration, anti-crime, and keeping Turkey out of the EU. Just before the van Gogh killing, a poll in a local left-wing paper, *De Volkskrant*, said that Wilders's support could equal about nine seats in the lower house of the Parliament, the Tweede Kamer.[5]

I met with Geert Wilders a few months later in my office at the *Washington Times* in Washington, D.C. He told me the disconcerting story of being kept under twenty-four-hour guard by police authorities because of continuing death threats from Dutch Islamists against him and his fellow party members. He can visit his wife only occasionally in secret locations, and then only under constant and heavy police protection.

But Wilders continues to travel around Holland and around the world, trying to alert people to the Islamist danger and to help organize a credible defense for his country and its culture. He explained to me that in Holland and in Europe, opposition to radical Islam—at an intellectual and policy level—is not as developed as it is in some circles in the United States. He was in Washington and New York to meet with journalists, government officials, and anti–Islamist terrorism experts who might assist him.

Wilders is no crank or racist. He is a decent, civilized family man who until recently was indistinguishable from millions of other Europeans. He is like so many other Europeans I have met and befriended in my travels. He was the kind of person with whom I instinctively feel a bond—a fellow member in a civilization that respects the individual, is tolerant of other religions, and wants nothing more than to live and let live.

Wilders is well educated, soft-spoken, and earnest. And that day in my office, he was afraid. But his fear did not stop him from acting boldly and speaking out in public. His palpable fear did not deafen him to the call of duty. I felt humbled in his presence.

Even outside my office door (which is well within our heavily secured newspaper headquarters), Wilders's guards maintained their watch. I couldn't help thinking, as I watched his tall, lonely figure walk down the corridor, accompanied by his guards, that he reminded me of the Victor Laszlo character in the 1942 film *Casablanca*. Laszlo, too, roamed the world—always in danger of arrest or execution—trying to provide leadership to the anti-Nazi struggle. But Geert Wilders's job, and the job of so many other politicians and ordinary citizens across Europe, is not an easy one. There is no clean and sweet way to rally a nation and a continent to its own defense against radical Islamists who live among them. The London *Times*, reporting on Wilders's political efforts, published a survey that indicated that 40 percent of the Dutch population "hope that Muslims no longer feel at home in the Netherlands."

An interesting footnote to Wilders's efforts is his standing in Dutch polls. Before the van Gogh assassination, Wilders's support stood at 6 percent. After the assassination, it jumped to 20 percent. And it has risen despite the fact that security concerns restrict his ability to campaign in the usual way.

The Dutch people are not alone in fearing a real threat to their culture and way of life. Even before the van Gogh killing—but six months after the slaughter of hundreds of Russian children in Beslan at the hands of Islamist terrorists—an Ipsos-Reid poll in Italy showed that 48 percent of Italians believed that a "clash of civilizations" between Islam and the West was under way and that Islam was "a religion more fanatical than any other."[6]

But it is not as simple as that. In December 2004, in Marseilles, two thousand people marched through the city denouncing violence against women, particularly in the immigrant-dominated communities. The protest was against Islamic "obscurantism" and "fundamentalism" that "imprisons women." But at the head of the demonstration was a group of Muslim women who called themselves "*Ni Putes ni Soumises*" (neither whores nor submissive).

The London *Times* described how the movement to protect Muslim women has developed chapters across the continent of Europe:

> The movement is supported by a mainstream opinion that has recently abandoned political correctness and wants to halt the inroads of Islam. From Norway to Sicily, governments, politicians, and the media are laying aside doctrines of diversity and insisting that "Islamism," as the French call the fundamentalist form that pervades the housing estates, is incompatible with Europe's liberal values. Even elite left wing French intellectuals, such as the commentator Jacques Julliard, said . . . that the left's longstanding tolerance had been used as "an agent for the penetration of Islamic intolerance."[7]

The struggle in Europe and the West is not against a race, religion, or nationality. It is against an attitude and conduct. Ultimately, of course, it will be the decent, civilized, non-jihadist Muslims who must reclaim their religion from those who would hijack it for unspeakable purposes.

Even Sweden is reacting against Muslim immigration and radical Islamist violence and cultural hostility. Because of Sweden's exceedingly liberal asylum immigration laws, Muslims now make up 25 percent of the southern town of Malmö. Each such asylum immigrant may bring spouses, brothers, and grandparents with him. A majority of Muslim students fail to graduate from the Swedish high schools. Unemployment for Muslims in Malmö runs to 90 percent, and predictably, the Muslim parts of the city are hostile to native Swedes. Ambulances cannot go into these parts without police escort. And then the ambulance attendants are told by angry crowds which patients they can take and which must be left behind.

Swedes set fire to Malmö's main mosque in 2004. When the fire-fighters arrived, they were pelted with stones by Swedish locals who wanted to keep the fire burning.[8]

It is not surprising that European leaders—despite their former commitment to multiculturalism—are beginning to respond to such popular fears about radical Islam. Politicians enjoy receiving praise from prominent left-wing academics and intellectuals, but voters' attitudes tend to be more persuasive in the long run. It is precisely this healthy democratic process that gives me reasonable hope that European governments will rally to the common defense of Western culture.

After the van Gogh murder, even the insufferable Dominique de Villepin—France's former secretary of state and President Bush's bête noire during the Iraq War, and after the French rejection of the EU constitution, the prime minister—ordered, as secretary of the interior, the deportation of foreign imams who supported wife beating. That same week, Prime Minister Jean-Pierre Raffarin called on French-based satellite company Eutelsat to stop transmitting the Lebanese station al Manor. Raffarin said al Manor's inflammatory anti-Semitic programming, which accused Israel of deliberately disseminating AIDS in Arab nations, was "incompatible with French values."[9]

Other senior politicians and media elites in Europe are talking in language that sounds less like the usual multiculturalism of Brussels bureaucrats and Sorbonne academics and more like my friend Pat Buchanan's discussion of culture wars.

The *Guardian*, the most stridently leftist of Britain's major newspapers, warned in its lead editorial of December 10, 2004, that in "Europe's faltering attempts to try to engage with its Muslim citizens, the lesson of recent years—intensified since 9/11, the war in Iraq and the Madrid train bombings—is that Muslims in France, Germany, the Netherlands and Britain must be taken more seriously by their governments, though not just by their police and security services."

The London *Times* had led the previous week with an article titled "Stoned to death: Why Europe is starting to lose faith in Islam." The first sentence: "Islamic fundamentalism is causing a clash of civilizations between liberal democracies and Muslims." I have yet to see such a lead in even conservative American newspapers.

In the weeks leading up to Christmas in 2004, Germans, from their chancellor on down, made public statements that in America would be scandalously, politically incorrect career killers. Chancellor Gerhard Schröder himself warned of "a conflict of cultures" and said Muslims "must clearly and without misunderstanding demonstrate that they accept our legal order and democratic rules." He went on to insist that "our willingness to integrate [Muslims into Germany] corresponds to a willingness to be integrated on the part of those who come here." Thus, the chancellor argued, Muslim immigrants must learn German: "Without linguistic abilities, no integration and no dialogue can take place."

Interior Minister Otto Schily issued a somewhat sharper warning to Islamic fundamentalists: "If you love death so much, then it can be yours."[10]

Edmund Stoiber—the leader of the opposition Christian Social Union (a conservative, Bavarian-based party) and one of the most popular politicians in Germany[11]—led his party caucus in an end-of-the-year unanimous vote against Turkish EU membership, for cutting welfare benefits for foreigners who won't integrate, and against "Islamist head scarves." Stoiber called on young Germans to "reclaim traditional German values." Angela Merkel, leader (and probably future chancellor) of the Christian Democratic Union (the national conservative party), announced that the multicultural society was a failure.

It might not be surprising for conservatives like Stoiber and Merkel to say these things, but it is very surprising indeed when Social Democrat Helmut Schmidt—chancellor from 1974 to 1982 and one of the fathers of the Turkish guest worker program—tells the *Hamburger Abendblatt* newspaper, "The concept of multiculturalism is difficult to make fit with a democratic society. . . . [It had been a mistake] that during the 1960s we brought guest workers from foreign cultures into the country. . . . [The cultural problems stemming from that mistake] could be overcome only by authoritarian governments."

Safter Cinar, spokesman for the Berlin and Brandenburg Turkish Association, responded harshly to the former chancellor: "Multiculturalism is not an option, it's not an ideology or a concept, it is a reality."[12] That seems to draw the line rather bluntly.

Meanwhile, in Britain, the early months of 2005 saw a battle between the governing Labour Party and the opposition Tory Party over which could be tougher on immigration. After the Tories took out a full-page advertisement in the *Sunday Telegraph* calling for limits on immigration, quotas for asylum seekers, curbs on work permits, and a promise of "round-the-clock security at ports."[13] Prime Minister Tony Blair of the Labour Party announced that only English-speaking applicants with proper work skills would be permitted to enter and settle in Britain.

During the election campaign, Islamic political power appeared on more than one occasion. There were, for example, Muslim protests against Oona King, a half-black and half-Jewish Labour member of Parliament (from a part of London formerly heavily Jewish, now heavily Muslim), which appeared to be targeted, in part, at her ethnicity. She was defeated in the election by George Galloway, who was a vocal opponent of the Iraq War and who has been accused of being a friend of Saddam Hussein and profiting from the UN's Oil for Food program.

There were also efforts by an organization called the Muslim Public Affairs Committee, which called for "political jihad." Reportedly, the Committee's stated purpose was to "eliminate all pro-Israeli Zionist MPs from power" and it referred to one member of Parliament as a "Zionist scumbag" who represented "Tel Aviv South."[14] The political elite in Britain largely tried to ignore such Islamic fascism, especially since many on the left accepted it as a political rebuke to Prime Minister Tony Blair's support for the Iraq War. Blair and his Labour Party went on to win the election, but with a much reduced majority in Parliament.

Such political accommodation aside, British public opinion seems headed in a more right-wing direction on Islamic immigration. The British newspaper *Mail on Sunday* released a poll in the first week of February 2005 reporting that 78 percent of Britons thought that immigration rules were not "tough enough." One in five Britons wanted a permanent end to any immigration—from anywhere by anyone. And most astoundingly, 70 percent disagreed with the proposition that Britain needed *any* foreign workers. This last point would be a surprise to probably every British government economist of the last fifty years. If this poll is anywhere near an accurate reflection of British opinion,[15] it could have major implications for Britain's, if not Europe's, future economic policy.

Less than a week after immigration began to dominate Blair's reelection campaign, Denmark held its national election. The incumbent prime minister Anders Fogh Rasmussen's center-right coalition government—composed of Rasmussen's Liberal Party, a coalition of conservative parties, and the far-right Danish People's Party—handily won reelection.

According to Agence France-Presse, "Denmark's immigration policy, perhaps the most restrictive in Europe, is believed especially to have drawn many voters to Rasmussen." The French press service report went on to quote a nineteen-year-old student supporter of Rasmussen: "Denmark has so far given too much financial support to immigrants. We simply have to keep some people out, and this government knows how to do it," the student said at a packed auditorium of enthusiastic student supporters of the government.

The news report quoted a Pakistani law student as well: "The whole climate is more hostile due to the government and the anti-immigrant rhetoric. There's no doubt people say things today they would have been criticized for ten years ago."

If 2004 was the year of Islamic shock in Europe, spring 2005 seemed to be the reaction—when practical European politicians begin to shift their policy and their rhetoric to respond to the public's correct assessment of the Islamic threat.

Beyond the politicians, it is now clear that the mandarins of the European academic/bureaucratic citadels are no longer as smugly complacent, politically correct, and disconnected from the practical considerations of life as they once were. Just as 2004 was the year that the man and woman in the European street and workaday politicians began to shift their thinking away from the grand old ideal of a multicultural Europe, so too, in the loftiest reaches of European universities and senior governmental bureaucracies, there is noticeable, even flagrant, doubt about the utility of multiculturalism and the underlying principles that have formed European policy and law as they relate to immigration and citizenship.

In the summer of 2004, after the Madrid bombing but before the horrors of Beslan or the shock of van Gogh's assassination, the cream of Europe's academic and bureaucratic elite met at St. Antony's College, Oxford University, to participate in a rarefied symposium called "Muslims in Europe post September 11th" under the joint auspices of Oxford and Princeton Universities.

The discussion was probably not much different from what was said in the Kremlin in the waning years of the old Soviet empire. Of course, a minority of true believers recited the old dogmas in a highly formalized, almost ritualistic manner. But much more interesting and more prevalent were the honest expressions that multiculturalism might be failing the reality test of actual life in Europe. These doubts—stripped of their academic trappings—are actually quite poignant, and a sign of hope that at the highest levels of leadership and thought in Europe, common sense and intellectual honesty are breaking through.

Sweden has been a European leader in advancing multiculturalism, Muslim immigration, and asylum seeking, but at the Oxford conference, Mona Sahlin, then the Swedish minister for democracy and integration, began her analysis with the concession that "a lively and polarized debate is under way on whether multiculturalism as a basis for policy is a condition enabling the ethnic and cultural diversity that exists in today's societies to function, or whether, on the contrary, it risks contributing to serious tensions and conflicts." She further conceded that multiculturalism as a government policy is seen by much of the public as a "threat to one's own side."

Sahlin noted that in accord with the dictates of multiculturalism, the prevalent government policy view has been to accept and protect immigrant customs "even if they conflict with the views and rules of the host country." She described the opposing policy as a "forced assimilation of the immigrants into a uniform, homogeneous host country culture." She then admitted that over the last decade, the former policies "almost consistently in practice have proved to be less positive than had been hoped for and expected."

Instead, she approvingly cited a study that concluded that such multicultural government policies "lead to a division of society into static, incompatible ethnic groups which hinders people's development instead of helping to advance it. People no longer actually feel personally and deeply involved in policies that are based on the broader interpretation of multiculturalism. People's identity is balkanized. Multiculturalism has come to be understood as something for immigrants, something devoid of interest for citizens in general or for the country."

Sahlin concluded, "If cultural differences are over-emphasized, we risk division and decay. If cultural differences are turned into ideology, the cohesiveness of the general social community may be threatened.... There is a danger in stressing the factors that separate us rather than those we have in common, that ethnic conflicts will be stirred up."

Another member of the panel, the University of London's distinguished scholar Sami Zubaida, reviewed sociological studies of indigenous British and Dutch reaction to immigrant Muslims. He noted that the public distinguished between the 60 to 70 percent of Muslims who were not fundamentalists and the 30 to 40 percent who were. The negative public attitudes against Muslims in Britain are focused on the conduct and attitude of the fundamentalists. "It is important to understand that in fact here you haven't got the traditional racist, xenophobic attitude against foreigners, that you've got the association with in your own history of Europe."

This is quite an important point and concession. For too long, European elites in government, the media, and the university have explained away negative public attitudes about Muslim immigrants as racism and xenophobia. That argument might have been plausible if only a handful of the public on the hard right mumbled their discontent. But as public concern about radical Muslims has entered all sectors of European opinion, the old argument doesn't stand up. It is important to see senior academics, the liberal elite, admit that decent Europeans are not racists because they fear the conduct of radical Muslims.

Stefano Allievi of the University of Padova suggested that multiculturalism will not resolve disputes between Muslims and Europeans. Short of genuine cultural integration of immigrants (which he supports), he believes that a civilizational clash between Islam and the West is likely to happen within Europe.

This theme was picked up by another prominent Italian academic, Mario Nordio of the Università Ca' Foscari di Venezia, who pointed out that "the Muslim population wasn't planned in Europe." The Muslim influx led first to "diversity," then to separate cultures; it did not lead to cultural assimilation.

A particularly fascinating insight was raised by one of Denmark's leading Islamic scholars, Jakob Skovgaard-Petersen of the University of Copenhagen. He pointed out that while Europe is governmentally integrating through the European Union, its people are unified only nationally—Danes remain Danish and read Danish newspapers, Swedes remain Swedish and read Swedish newspapers—and think and relate publicly in such terms. But in the Arab world, the opposite is the case. There is no coordinated pan-Arab or Muslim governmental coordination, yet Arabs and Muslims think as a non-national group and gain their news through al Jazeera and its like. This creates "an imbalance in both places" and is a source of legitimate worry.

Moreover, he confessed, the European public is increasingly aware of the problem of Islamic separatism and is blaming the government and academic elites: "People like myself and others who have been writing about Islam in Denmark are suddenly criticized because we are said to be politically correct and so on and so forth. This is an Americanization or polarization of the debate. Certain new groups of intellectuals and journalists have come up who are extremely skeptical about the public knowledge of Islam, which is considered too apologetic. I would say there is not only an Islamophobia, but there is a kind of growing Islamistphobia."

That last line is important. It suggests the same point made by Professor Zubaida. The professor uses Islamophobia to refer to old-fashioned hatred or fear of foreigners who happen to be Muslim. But Islamistphobia is a fear of the ideas and conduct of radical Muslims. While only a racist would hate someone for the color of his skin or his last name, decent, honorable people have a duty to oppose ideas and conduct they judge harmful to their civilization. It is this rising Islamist-phobia that is getting the attention of the European elites.

Another participant at the Oxford symposium, Anja Rudiger, executive coordinator of the United Kingdom's European Monitoring Centre on Racism and Xenophobia, would appear to be a true believer, dedicated to the old multiculturalist policies. Her comments are noteworthy for their ideological fervor and their separation from actual British politics. She started out with a careful analytical observation:

> It does seem that after 9/11 religion has almost surpassed race as the prime side of conflict. While it is no longer acceptable to use skin colour as an immutable attribute to distinguish people, it is now religion and culture that have gained currency as markers of seemingly natural signs of difference.
>
> European Muslims used to be perceived as racial, ethnic or national minorities; now their identity is increasingly marked by their faith. Moreover, religion is often perceived as synonymous with culture.
>
> This process of designating another group as the "other," maybe the European "other," at first sight seems similar for racial groups and religious groups. But if religion now is this new

"other," or specifically Islam is the new "other," what is the specificity of religious discrimination?

Dr. Rudiger went on to make an important distinction between discrimination of religious "groups" and discrimination of religious (or cultural) "practices," which, while they overlap, are two different types of discrimination. While as a strict multiculturalist, she doesn't advocate discrimination against dangerous cultural conduct or ideas, she is at least realistic enough to note that the public sees it differently, and she frets that the European politicians might respond to these distinctions: "There's been a debate in the [European] Convention about whether to include, as one of the paragraphs of the constitution, a reference to Europe's Christian tradition. I don't think this will actually happen, but that there's even the possibility that the Convention would discuss this does show that there are severe problems at EU level when it comes to the issue of religious diversity." Those words were uttered in mid-2004. In January 2005, a reference to Christianity was in fact included in the draft constitution, although admittedly in a watered-down version. She went on to express opposition to European and British trends toward tighter immigration laws for Muslims. As mentioned above, those trends have heightened in importance in British and Danish electoral politics.

Maleiha Malik of King's College, London, a jurist who specializes in United Kingdom and European Union anti-discrimination law and who is of self-described "Muslim allegiance," has written on the need to redefine loyalty to British democracy in ways that reduce traditional concepts of nationalism and patriotism. But even she conceded at the Oxford symposium, "There are legitimate security concerns, which have to be acknowledged in any reasonable debate on the post–September 11 situation. It has to be recognized that the state, the United States, and the European Union member states will have to undertake heavier policing of the Muslim community similar to the heavier policing of the Irish community during the period of attacks by the IRA in the UK." One could only wish that George Bush's secretary of transportation, Norman Mineta, who vehemently opposes passenger profiling, held the same view as this quite radical British Muslim law professor.

Dr. Malik went on, "Too often Muslims have expected the majority to accommodate their needs without being willing to accept that they must adjust themselves to the basic values of liberal constitutionalism and a respect for individual rights which are part of liberal democracies. There are some who may think these values are incompatible with Islam. However, there are others who [disagree]."

Professor Gilles Kepel is head of the postgraduate department of Arab and Muslim Worlds at Paris's elite, anti-American Institut d'études Politiques in Paris. He reviewed the happy anti-American solidarity that French Muslims and the indigenous French share over the unpopular Iraq War for the Oxford symposium. He also noted that many European Muslims have integrated well and have become "British, French, Belgian and even German citizens." Then he delivered a more sobering analysis:

Yet alongside these structural evolutions, some disturbing phenomena have shown up over the last few years that may be the spark that ignites the immigrant suburbs, the inner cities and the projects of Europe's big cities, as well as schools and high schools where students of Muslim origin are sometimes a majority.

First of all, as the many arrests in Germany, in France, in Spain, in Great Britain and in Belgium have shown, jihadist networks, we mentioned that this morning, linked to Osama bin Laden, have found recruits in Europe from "Londonistan," as we'll call the British capital . . . which harbors the most radical groups and the most extreme Internet websites, to Hamburg, where the operational cell responsible for 9/11 was pulled together, and passing through various and sundry charitable organizations, the list is long of militant networks that worry the European police. . . . They fear that little groups of "sleepers," even though they have no popular following, may carry out terrorist acts . . . sowing panic in European cities and pitting Muslims against non-Muslims in a sort of doomsday scenario of religious and social wars.

Professor Kepel goes on to say that

One has to admit that among educated young Muslims in Europe, the reaction to the attacks on New York and Washington has translated into a sort of exacerbation of religious identity, as if to proclaim that Islam itself will not be put in the dock. We have seen the [extreme Salafist movement grow in] influence [which] has heightened tensions in some schools where the style of life they advocate is viewed by the teachers as a permanent challenge to the values of the European education system.

Note how his analysis contradicts fundamental principles of European multicultural integration. Not only are the poor, illiterate European Muslims a threat, but "educated young Muslims" are also threats to European culture. If the most pampered, the best and brightest, of European Islam are turning against European culture and democracy,

then multicultural policies as they have been carried out for a generation are at a dead end.

It is worth noting that while Americans think we are fighting the
war on terrorism more vigorously than the Europeans, liberal Europeans are both more alive to the cultural and immigration front of the
Islamist threat and more able to speak bluntly about the danger. It
would seem that political correctness is a more intimidating mentality
in America.

From Italy to Germany to Denmark to Britain to France to Holland
and Sweden, from angry people in the street to local politicians to
national leaders to the mandarin theoreticians of European culture,
2004 was the year in which the continent of Europe finally realized the
potentially mortal threat in its midst—the first step toward recovery.

CHAPTER FIVE

The Deracination
of the West

I T IS CLEAR THAT EUROPE AND THE United States failed to anticipate or notice the problem of radical Islam. Until September 11, 2001, in the United States, and November 2004 (after the assassination of Theo van Gogh) in Europe, the West made no real response to Islamic threats. Even now, the solutions the West embraces could be the wrong ones. This raises the question of how so successful a civilization could make such disastrous decisions until shocked into action by terrorism and growing extremist populations within their own borders.

It was the Europeans' plan that Muslims take the nasty jobs that indigenous Europeans didn't want. The Europeans never imagined that their "invited guests" would compete for cultural dominance and come to control entire cities. Already, more than 40 percent of Rotterdam's population is Muslim. And over the next fifty to one hundred years, if the population trends continue they will lead to the supplanting of indigenous Europeans—indeed, to their virtual extinction—by Muslims.

Europe's future is in danger because Europe has forgotten its past. In the Middle Ages, Europeans held a healthy respect, even fear and awe, of the power and vigor of Islamic culture. From the time of Islam's conquest of North Africa, Spain, the Holy Land, and the Near East, right up until the siege of Vienna in 1683, when the Polish king John III defeated Grand Vizier Kara Mustafa's besieging army, Europeans knew about the clash of civilizations.

Europeans gradually forgot the danger and the formidable underpinnings of Islamic culture, as the Islamic world fell into decline and the West rose. But the brief period when European technology overwhelmed Muslim cultural confidence has come to an end—just when Europeans have come to rely on the Muslim labor in their midst.

The West miscalculated when it saw Muslim immigrants as similar to other ethnic immigrants—bright, hopeful, hardworking, and eager to become an integral part of their host country's successful culture. While this might well describe many Muslim immigrants, growing numbers of other Muslim immigrants, and even second- and third-generation Muslims in Europe (and to a lesser extent in America), do not see Western culture as successful or want to identify themselves with it; they do not want to be shaped in the Western mold. The usual methods of encouraging integration—education, dialogue, economic support, respect for the immigrants' special needs—is not working. It is not working because many Muslims don't want to integrate—they want to dominate.

The Europeans who invited the massive Muslim immigration made another mistake. They failed to realize that Europe has grown culturally weak, and they failed to recognize how vigorous Islamic culture is. The gradual process of Islam's transformation of Europe went unnoticed until multiculturalism was imposed on the common people, and they reacted against these fundamental changes in their countries—changes that they would never have agreed to at the outset.

One reason that it took Western leaders so long to notice is that there is a growing class of Western elites—international businesspeople, bureaucrats, government officials, journalists—who feel only a tenuous connection to their various countries, who are more committed to globalization than to their national cultures, and who identify more readily with business associates and activities than with civil, political, and cultural aspects of a specific nation. Any plausible plan to resist the Islamist threat will inevitably entail some disconnection between nations. But the globalist project requires ever more connections, irrespective of other factors. Thus, there is an emerging conflict of interest between the international globalists and common men and women trying to protect their culture, whether that culture is in Borneo or Berlin, Angola or Antwerp.

So what does the West do with a growing population of Islamists who have no desire to integrate into Western civilization—especially when some of these Muslims are true jihadists, when many Muslims would protect jihadists, and when many Muslims say they want to take over Europe by expanding Muslim population and culture?

It is increasingly likely that such a threat cannot be defeated while the West continues to adhere to its deeply held values—as it currently understands them—of tolerance, the right to privacy, the right even to advocate sedition, and the right to equal protection under the law. The day is upon us when the West will have to decide which it values more: granting these rights and tolerance to those who wish to destroy us, or the survival of Western civilization. And this is another reason the West has been slow to react—because reacting violates its own values.

But there may be a moral escape hatch. The West's current understanding of these great values has changed dramatically since World War

II, when Franklin Delano Roosevelt's America and Winston Churchill's Britain led the war against fascism. Modern-day Americans and Europeans might be surprised to read about how their recent, admired, democratic ancestors interpreted those values when confronted with mortal danger.

But before we can understand why they acted the way they did, we need to understand the historic tracks of Western thinking that have brought the West to the brink of cultural collapse, its current vulnerability to Islamist terror strikes, and its failure to act as FDR and Churchill did.

DEADLY POLITICAL CORRECTNESS

British novelist and World War II veteran George MacDonald Fraser writes in his recent memoir *The Light's on at Signpost* that the present generation of his fellow Britons

> regard themselves as a completely liberated society, when the fact is that they are less free than any generation before them since the Middle Ages. Indeed, there may never have been such an enslaved generation, in thrall to hang-ups, taboos, restrictions, and oppressions unknown to their ancestors.
>
> They won't believe, of course, that they don't know what freedom is, and that we were freer by far fifty years ago. . . . We could say what we liked; they can't. We were not subject to the aggressive pressure of special interest minority groups; they are. We had no worries about race or sexual orientation; they have. . . . We could and did differ from fashionable opinion with impunity, and would have laughed political correctness to scorn."[1]

Most people over the age of forty-five can probably remember when there were no political correctness "police" constantly trying to prevent people from expressing themselves in normal ways. They can probably remember when left-wing academic gibberish didn't seem to intrude into national policy and daily life. To such people, like me, it is curious how all these odd intrusions have come to dominate society. Indeed, in Europe, these hostile ideas have become formal national and EU policies. How did this come about? Part of the answer lies in how average people simply reacted to the dramatic events of the last hundred years. But without being too conspiratorial-minded, elements of the intellectual and academic left have given the process a helping hand.

The late professor Robert Nisbet once shrewdly observed, "We live, it has often been said, under the spell of ideas, good or bad, true or false. We may think we are responding directly to events and changes in the histories of institutions, but we aren't; we are responding to these events and changes as they are made real or assimilable to us by ideas already in our heads."[2]

Put yourself in the mind of a typical European reflecting on the twentieth century. The reflections would center on two world wars of shocking human slaughter and chaos. It is no wonder that Europeans— and some Americans—have been losing faith in the West's history, institutions, religion, and values, losing faith in the promise of Western civilization itself (even though the victors in both those wars thought that Western civilization was at stake). The West's loss of confidence has led us down a path of estrangement from our civilization that, if left unobstructed, will lead to continued decay and decline.

To many Europeans, the world wars understandably discredited nationalism as a largely negative and destructive sentiment. They also understandably discredited notions of cultural and racial superiority or cultural and racial pride as a repulsive atavistic mentality that led to the Holocaust and the slaughter of six million Jews, as well as millions of others.

These authentic popular reactions to recent history have been fought over and exploited by intellectuals, academics, and politicians for almost a century now. Multiculturalism and political correctness, though championed by many people as sincere efforts to improve society, had their origins in a breakaway Marxist movement that intended to defeat capitalism not by challenging its economic principles but by undermining the traditional culture that supported it. These theories were centered on the Frankfurt School, a group of intellectuals that moved from Germany to America in the 1930s. Among its more famous members were Herbert Marcuse, Theodor Adorno, and Walter Benjamin.[3] Their influence would be felt in the radical New Left of the 1960s and would eventually filter down into popular culture. As their ideas spread, even old-style liberals were not safe from politically correct multiculturalism.

The renowned liberal novelist Saul Bellow outraged multiculturalists when he asserted: "Find me the Tolstoy of the Zulus, or the Proust of the Papuans, and I would be happy to read him." Consequently, this great liberal voice was falsely charged with racism. Another lion of twentieth-century liberalism, Arthur Schlesinger Jr., quite bravely gave us an early warning, in his 1992 book *The Disuniting of America*, that multiculturalism was culturally dangerous. This "cult of ethnicity," as he called multiculturalism, "could destroy the nation."[4]

The reality is that the cultural Marxists and "critical thinkers" have been stunningly successful over the last half-century. While most people have been going about their daily lives, the multiculturalists have effectively changed the way a large segment of Europeans and Americans think.

But it has to be admitted that they had fertile ground to plow. Racism was and is a disgraceful attitude. Colonialism was largely exploitative of non-whites around the world. Women had been denied a fair place in society. And the uncontrolled competitive and acquisitive instincts of European nation-states had unleashed the horrors of two world wars.

Politicians and professors who called for tolerance, peacefulness, and fairness to all peoples were destined to find a receptive public in light of all that had gone on before. But slowly, what seemed like reasonable criticism of a flawed Western civilization mentally evolved, for millions of Westerners, from constructive criticism to cultural self-loathing.

Anyone who suggested that this was all going too far was accused of being an advocate of the old, bad ways of racism, imperialism, colonialism, sexism, and other "isms." The sensible middle found it easier to keep quiet than to risk having such terrible charges laid against them. This was particularly the case for politicians. For journalists and academics, expressing any reservations about the multicultural and politically correct agenda would bar them from even being hired into the profession—at least, into its elite precincts.

As early as 1964, James Burnham was diagnosing the problem in his book *Suicide of the West*. He noted the contraction of Western civilization around the globe (largely through the end of Western colonialism) and pointed out that "this contraction cannot be accounted for by the material power of any agency external to Western civilization; . . . it cannot be accounted for by any Western deficiency in material power or resources; . . . it must therefore derive from structural or non-material factors."

Burnham diagnosed what he thought accounted for these "structural or non-material factors." They were a set of ideas that dominated certain sectors of the West. He wrote that "what Americans call 'liberalism' is the ideology of Western suicide." Burnham was no radical or cheap political point scorer. He was a serious and respected thinker, and wove a subtle argument: "I do not mean that liberalism is 'the cause' of the contraction. The whole problem of historical causation is in any case too complex for simple assertions. I mean, rather, in part, that liberalism has come to be the typical verbal systemization of the process of Western contraction and withdrawal; that liberalism motivates and justifies the contraction and reconciles us to it."[5]

So for decades, the West has been losing faith in itself and justifying that loss of faith as either not a problem or perhaps even a good thing. But we have reached a stage when it is most clearly not a good thing. In the strangest possible irony, the threat of radical Islam is giving the West a second chance to regain its faith in itself. Left unchallenged, it is a second chance we almost certainly never would have given ourselves.

If we truly don't value Western civilization, we should be willing, perhaps eager, to let our children, grandchildren, and great-grandchildren live under different conditions. Some people even argue that the declining birthrate in Europe is the physical manifestation of that mentality. Enjoy the maximum material comfort and don't even bother to curse our notional progeny with existence in our terrible civilization, which is racist, sexist, homophobic, materialist, and imperialist—all things that flowed from four hundred years of world domination by the West.

The irony is that we have been so dominant that there has been nothing to measure ourselves against—except our own ideals. Certainly the Chinese, Hindu, and Muslim cultures between 1600 and 1950 were not significant enough to be noticed or cared about by most people in the West.

Measuring ourselves against our own ideals, we found ourselves wanting. Indeed, since the Enlightenment, one of our central ideals has been to question authority. But given the dominance of the West and the weakness of the rest of the world over the last three or four centuries, the only authorities worth questioning were our own: kings, Christianity, capitalism, materialism, white people, and even unprecedented democratic politics that nonetheless excluded the very weakest from participation. All our own institutional authorities were the natural and vulnerable targets of our civilization's relentless self-questioning.

We have turned our Western-trained intellect, with its rapacious analytical skills, on our own civilization and found little to withstand our harsh and haughty standards of perfection. We have, in essence, been performing acts of auto-da-fé on our own values. In our extraordinarily judgmental minds, we find that we have committed heresies against our Platonic ideals. Our institutions—the earthly, inadequate forms of our ideals—are declared corrupt.

Left unchecked, the process could only end, as James Burnham said, in "the suicide of the West." When he wrote in 1964, multiculturalism did not have a name, but under his more general term of "liberalism" he described its features and noted that "the most important practical consequence of the guilt encysted in the liberal ideology and psyche is this: that the liberal, and the group, nation or civilization infected by liberal doctrine and values, are morally disarmed before those whom the liberal regards as less well off than himself."[6]

Now, suddenly, as if from nowhere, arises a real, likely alternative to our self-despised civilization—radical Islam—and Burnham's analysis would imply that liberal guilt could morally disarm us in the face of the danger that radical Islam threatens.

But how bad do all the shortcomings of Western civilization look if the alternative is radical Islam right in the heart of Europe or America? If current birthrates continue, if current EU cultural policies continue, if current multicultural sensibilities continue to deny Western institutions any protection and special respect, if current unthinking tolerance of the intolerant continues, if current thinking in Europe (and to a substantial extent in America) doesn't change, Western values and lifestyles will be supplanted in Europe by the values of radical Islam.

If Western civilization has kept women down with its sexism, how does it compare with Islamic civilization? If Western civilization has asserted cultural imperialism on the Third World, how does it compare with Islamic influence on the Third World? If we still discriminate against homosexuals, how does it compare with how the Islamic world treats homosexuals? If the West has been corrupted by materialism, how does it compare with the material standards of Islamic societies? It all comes down to this: If the choice is a flawed Western civilization or an impending fundamentalist Islamist civilization, which one do you want to live in?

I expect that the intellectuals (and the government officials and elite media whom they affect) will be the most resistant to a rational defense of our culture and civilization, because it takes an overdeveloped love of one's own bright ideas to lead one to truly ludicrous conclusions. One has to overthink oneself to arrive at truly deep levels of irrationality. A normally intelligent, healthy person sees the world he or she lives in fairly accurately and acts rationally within that world.

The people least encumbered by the hundred-year history of anti-Western thinking are those who have least imbibed it—still-practicing Christians and Jews and other regular, common, working people of Europe and America. I expect to see a renaissance of belief in Western civilization to come, more or less, from the middle and bottom up, from popular thought, not elite thought. This is where the shock at the van Gogh assassination, at the Madrid train bombings, at the Beslan slaughter of the innocents, and at the increasingly publicized cultural arrogance of radical European Muslims is beginning to have its effect in Europe. And this is where the outrage and revealed danger of September 11, 2001, remains fresh in American minds.

Because the bedrock Western value of representative government remains, the West has an excellent chance of overcoming the irrational policies of Western elites and galvanizing itself to an effective defense of its culture and civilization.

In the next chapter, we'll see how the Western democracies galvanized themselves to defeat fascism in World War II, an experience with enormous lessons for us as we confront the new threat of Islamo-fascism.

CHAPTER SIX

Saving Democracy, 1940s Style

"WHEN ARE YOU GOING TO indict the seditionists?" Franklin Delano Roosevelt demanded of his attorney general, Francis Biddle, a few months after the attack on Pearl Harbor. Biddle sent Justice Department attorney William Maloney to convene a grand jury to do the president's bidding. A few months later, twenty-eight "native fascists" were indicted.[1]

But before Maloney could get to trial, Biddle fired him. The press accused Biddle of bowing to isolationist sentiments. The even-then liberal *Washington Post* ripped into Biddle in an editorial titled "Appeasement is Folly," in which the *Post* virtually accused the attorney general of cutting deals with Hitler when he fired Maloney.[2]

A few months later, FDR, impatient for Congress to pass wage and price control legislation, took to the radio airwaves, saying, "I ask Congress to take action by the first of October. Inaction on your part by that date will leave me with an inescapable responsibility to the people of this country to see to it that the war effort is no longer imperiled by threat of economic chaos." If Congress did not act, Roosevelt warned, "I shall accept the responsibility and I will act."[3] Such was the mood in Washington as America joined World War II.

Two years earlier, on the other side of the Atlantic, as France was falling to Hitler's blitzkrieg, King George VI had asked Winston Churchill to form a government. The *New Yorker*'s London correspondent, Mollie Panter-Downes, captured the mood in Britain's capital two weeks later on May 24, 1940:

> While the greatest battle in history is being fought on the other side of the Channel, which has suddenly shrunk in most people's minds to something no bigger than the Thames, an equally great revolution has been taking place here. In a single day so much constitutional ballast was heaved overboard in order to lighten the unwieldy ship for this swift and deadly new warfare that a number of revered statesmen must have positively writhed in their graves. If the British people had their way, several more—who were once revered but are now revealed in all their heavy guilt of irresponsibility for placing the country in its present critical peril—would shortly be joining them.
>
> Even the slowest minds in a race not famed for lightning perceptions have grasped at last, with anger and bitterness, the exact extent of that peril to which years of complacent leadership have brought them, and they are ready emotionally for the most drastic measures Mr. Churchill may choose to take. On the day the [Defence of the Realm] Act was passed empowering the Government to require all persons "to place themselves, their services, and their property at the disposal of His Majesty," a coster [street salesman of cheap items] on a donkey cart possibly summed up

the universal comment on the announcement of Britain's total mobilization when he shouted to a crony, "That's right! All in it together to knock 'is bleedin' block off!"

All in it they certainly are, donkey cart and Rolls-Royce alike. "There must be no laggards," warned Mr. Attlee [leader of the Labour Party and part of Churchill's coalition government]. "Victory is our goal. We must and shall attain it." Nobody doubts that to do so the Government will use its new powers, more complete than any government has held since Cromwell's time, to the utmost. The Englishman's home is no longer his castle but a place that can be commandeered at a moment's notice if the state needs it. Landowners must be prepared to give up their land; employers to close down their businesses or to carry on under government control, and perhaps at a loss; employees to change their jobs as they may be directed by the Ministry of Labour.[4]

To Americans in 2005, these government intrusions on civil liberties must sound strange—and yet, perhaps, not so strange. Recall your thoughts on September 11, 2001, when you were watching the Twin Towers collapsing on television, people jumping out of windows ninety stories up, and the Pentagon burning, its north face obliterated by the crashed airliner. Remember as you first became aware of the grim visage of Osama bin Laden and that thing called al Qaeda. Recall the beat of your heart as you held your wife, husband, or lover close, or looked down on your children's faces and worried about their physical safety.

If you can—and this may be harder—try to remember those moments in the days and weeks after September 11 when you didn't think as a Republican or Democrat, as a liberal or conservative, as a devout Christian or big-city agnostic, when you didn't think for or against George Bush. Remember when Jay Leno and David Letterman were afraid to make a joke about anything, when there were no civilian airplanes flying in America.

At those moments, would you have been angry if the FBI had announced that they were going to check public library records to see who had been checking out books on bomb-making and airplane boarding methods? Or, instead, would you have been beside yourself with anger if you heard on television that the FBI was not going to run down every possible lead to catch the terrorists before they blew up the White House, or your child's school?

The big question is whether you were irrational then, to want the government to do what it had to do in order to protect your family and your country from death and destruction—back when you were really afraid of the danger terrorists posed. Or are you irrational now, to be satisfied with the government doing less than it could to stop terrorism? Are you right to no longer be afraid of terrorism?

In England in 1940 and in America in 1942, no one doubted the reality of physical danger. In England, in particular, the expectation of imminent catastrophe was real. My parents, like many other Londoners, put off having children (even though they were well into their childbearing years) because they didn't see the point of bringing children into a world that Hitler might well be running within weeks. In 1942, Japanese on the American West Coast were rounded up and put in camps, on the fear that they would commit sabotage or send signals to the Japanese navy that might be lurking off the coast. According to accounts at the time, a Japanese torpedo had hit a beach in Santa Barbara, California. The physical danger of war was plenty real for Americans, too.

So it is worthwhile to take a look at what powers and authority the two great democracies, America and Britain, were prepared to grant their governments in order to make the most effective possible defense of their nations in the face of the great danger that threatened their survival.

The powers willingly granted to the governments of FDR and Winston Churchill would doubtlessly shock many Americans today. President Bush and British prime minister Tony Blair have been called fascists and seekers of unconstitutional powers for asking their legislatures for far less authority than their predecessors were willingly given just six decades ago, even though government as a whole has expanded greatly since World War II.

Both the law and common sense recognize that the greater the threatening danger, the more one may lawfully do to protect oneself. For example, it is a crime to commit trespass, theft, or burglary. But if it is necessary for the protection of your life to break into a house or take property that is not your own in order to fend off a potentially lethal attack, the principle of necessity exculpates the actor from any criminal liability.

Similarly, a constitutionally formed government may exercise greater powers, including diminutions of individual civil liberties in time of war, if such diminutions are deemed necessary for the collective defense. In ancient Roman law, the phrase was *inter arma silent leges*—"in time of war the laws are silent." And even under our own constitution, as Chief Justice William Rehnquist has noted, "there is some truth" in that maxim. In discussing the concept of civil liberties, the chief justice wrote, "It is not simply liberty, but civil liberty, of which we speak. The word 'civil,' in turn, is derived from the Latin word *civis*, which means 'citizen.' A citizen is a person owing allegiance to some organized government, and not a person in an idealized 'state of nature' free from any governmental restraint."

He went on to cite Judge Learned Hand, one of the greatest American jurists, in remarks delivered during World War II on the topic "The Spirit of Liberty": "A society in which men recognize no check upon their freedom soon becomes a society where freedom is the possession of only a savage few."[5]

I understand that many people do not believe America is in great jeopardy. I have made my case for the presence of an existential threat that hangs over our future as a nation and a civilization. In this chapter I simply want to describe the lengths America was prepared to go to during World War II, when there was a consensus that the nation was truly in danger. Britain, not having a Bill of Rights, went even further.

The overwhelming majority of Americans and Britons during World War II believed they were living in democracies.[6] Our parents and grandparents surely loved and cherished their peacetime liberties as much as we do today. They didn't feel oppressed by their governments; they felt protected. It is my argument that if our governments today had the same powers exercised by FDR and Churchill, we would not be violating the fundamental principles of democratic, constitutional government. I believe that we can use those standards embraced and exercised by the great liberal Franklin Delano Roosevelt and the near universally admired Winston Spencer Churchill during World War II as a benchmark for decent, liberal democratic governmental standards.

Neither government exercised all the powers it was granted, because some of the powers were not needed. It is likely that our governments today would not need to exercise all of those same powers, because some are either unnecessary or ineffective. On the other hand, we should be aware of the possibility that the American and British governments today might need to possess and exercise some powers not needed by our recent ancestors, because times, adversaries, and technologies have changed in the past six decades.

It is worth recalling that Studs Terkel memorably called World War II "the good war" because as he interviewed hundreds of GIs and their families many years after the war, they recalled that the struggle lifted them above their personal lives to fight on behalf of something they believed was greater than themselves. In the memories of those who lived through and fought in World War II, it was good despite the millions of deaths, the limitations on daily lives, the encroachment on peacetime liberties, and the arduousness of wartime life. It was good because the sacrifice was for a noble cause, for the perpetuation of America and the American way of life.

I would argue that the struggle against Islamist terrorism is an equally good war, and for the same reasons. I would also argue that we have just as great a responsibility to win our struggle against insurgent Islamist aggression as our parents and grandparents had to win World War II. There is no other cause so urgent. If we do not pay with our sacrifices now, we (and our children) will pay in greater losses later. We must be prepared to be just as ruthless and rational as the Greatest Generation was in defeating fascism.

As Eric Larrabee wrote in *Commander in Chief: Franklin Delano Roosevelt, His Lieutenants and Their War*:

> For all the atrocities the Axis perpetrated against civilians, and they were many, it was the peace-loving Anglo-Americans—once their blood lust was up—who proved to be utterly implacable in dealing destruction and death to the homes, wives and children of the men they faced in battle.

This was the route to which the President gave his powerful assent. The choice of it led a long way, longer perhaps than any other choice the Allies made. Their political objectives were implicit in the way they chose to fight.... That is, the total defeat of their enemies came first and determined the strategies employed to that end.[7]

Just as Britain and America's generals and admirals made no compromise to the imperative of total victory on the battlefield, so British and American political leaders, courts, and popular opinion let the requirements for victory define the powers of their government on the home front.[8] So what powers did the wartime Western allies—in particular, President Roosevelt's government—actually possess, and how did they exercise those powers?

WARTIME POWERS IN THE UNITED STATES DURING WORLD WAR II

Propaganda

In May 1942, naval intelligence intercepted Japanese communications indicating the date and time of an attack on Midway Island. Our government decided to make an inspirational documentary of the coming battle. Director John Ford was recruited to make the documentary while working for the Office of Strategic Services (OSS) Field Photographic Branch.[9]

Ford and his film crew were flown out to Midway on June 2, a day before the battle, to start shooting. They stayed throughout the battle, and Ford was even knocked unconscious by shrapnel from a Japanese bomb. After the battle, he was flown to Hollywood, where he edited the film at MGM studios.

According to one film critic, the result was a masterpiece of inspirational propaganda. Before the battle, the young soldiers are seen swimming, laughing, talking nervously in small groups. Then, sunrise and golden light pierce the clouds. Suddenly, Japanese Zeros come shooting out of the clouds. Battle scenes follow, but Ford is careful not to let the combat scenes seem too horrific. Heroic acts are caught on film, and when a squad of Marines hoists an American flag while under heavy enemy fire, our national anthem swells over the soundtrack.

Abruptly, the fighting stops and "stern" images of the aftermath unroll, including a funeral sequence in which the "determined faces of the survivors" watching the burial are on view for the film audience. The film ends with a record of the accomplishments of our men fighting in the battle, while an orchestration of "Over There" gets louder and the film fades to black.

Eleanor Roosevelt was said to have cried at the White House screening, and FDR proclaimed, "I want every mother in America to see this picture." Although originally intended to be screened just for the troops, the film was mass-released in five hundred movie theaters in America, on the president's order.[10]

During World War II, hundreds of Hollywood's top actors, directors, and production personnel were recruited by the federal government to make propaganda films and radio programs for distribution to the American public, as well as for our troops and for viewing abroad. While such Hollywood greats as John Ford, George Stevens, and Frank Capra willingly applied their talent for the propaganda efforts, the fact is that all of them were subordinate to a military or intelligence officer of the federal government. This was straight government propaganda targeted at the minds and hearts of the American public.

In the course of the war, the government's propaganda filmmaking rivaled Hollywood's in its complexity and the number of films produced. Of course, Hollywood was voluntarily producing reliable pro-American and pro-Allies films throughout the war as well. As war scholar Paul Fussell wrote, "The various outlets of popular culture behaved almost entirely as if they were creatures of their governments ... they spoke with one voice."[11]

Censorship

Just as the federal government had the authority to manufacture and distribute propaganda to advance an optimistic view of the war, it also had the authority to censor the press in order to suppress negative information. On December 8, 1941, FDR gave FBI director J. Edgar Hoover emergency authority to censor all news and control all communications going into or out of the country.[12] Initially, about twenty-six stories a day were censored.[13]

By December 18, 1941, the National Association of Broadcasters published its own wartime guide:

> DO NOT take chances with ad lib broadcasts ... an open microphone accessible to the general public constitutes a very real hazard in times of war.
>
> DO NOT broadcast personal observations on weather conditions. Watch sports broadcasts for this. A late night comment that "it's a fine clear night" might be invaluable information to the enemy.
>
> DO NOT broadcast any long list of casualties. This has been specifically forbidden.[14]

Within two months, federal regulations were enacted that set up a bureaucracy and official criteria to manage censorship. According to the Press Codes issued by the federal Office of Censorship on February 20, 1942, censorship covered troop movements and ship sinkings as well as:

- Reports of air raids
- The civil, military, industrial, financial or economic plans of the United States or its allies
- Criticism of equipment, appearance, physical condition or morale of the armed forces of the United States or any of its allies
- Any other matter . . . which might directly or indirectly bring aid or comfort to the enemy, or which might interfere with the national effort, or disparage the foreign relations of the United States or any anti-Axis nations.[15]

The reporting of rumor or atrocity stories was also outlawed, with publishers cautioned by the government that "the spread of rumors in such a way that they will be accepted as fact will render aid and comfort to the enemy. . . . Equal caution should be used in handling so-called atrocity stories."[16]

By the end of 1942, the Post Office had banned seventy newspapers under the Espionage Act. The anti-Semitic Father Charles Coughlin's newspaper, *Social Justice*, was censored. The newspaper of the Socialist Workers Party, the *Militant*, was banned. Even the annual shareholders' report of United States Steel for 1941 was censored to show production as "00,000 thousand tons."[17] By 1944, more than 500,000 pieces of private mail had been intercepted and held by the Office of Censorship, pursuant to the War Powers Act; letters, cables, telephone calls, and films were inspected.[18] The Enemy Alien Property Division of the Treasury Department confiscated any publication outright—even if it had been published by American citizens—if there was any credible evidence that it had been even partially funded by enemy funds. After Pearl Harbor, virtually all the publications of the German-American Bund were also confiscated.[19]

In Search of Subversion

In the years immediately prior to America's entry into the war, Congress passed laws that, collectively, authorized President Roosevelt to instruct the FBI to thoroughly investigate any possible or even vaguely suspected subversive activity. The Foreign Agents Registration Act of 1938, the Smith Act of 1940, and the Voorhis Act of 1941 were the grounds for Roosevelt's wartime domestic surveillance of American citizens whose political activity might lead them to serve the interests of opposing nations.20

Attorney General Robert Jackson described the targets and responsibility of the FBI's domestic intelligence activities as involving "steady surveillance over individuals and groups within the United States... which [are] ready to give assistance or encouragement in any form to invading or opposing ideologies."[21] In service of those wartime objectives, Roosevelt authorized the FBI to use wiretaps (without a warrant), surreptitious entries, and "champering" (secretly intercepting and reading private mail without consent).[22]

Between 1941 and 1943, the Justice Department's Special War Policies Unit, working on what then attorney general Biddle called "the post-investigative level," took extensive "action on the internal security front." These actions included interning thousands of enemy aliens and denaturalizing and deporting members of the German-American Bund, as well as prosecuting individuals for sedition, prosecuting foreign propaganda agents, and prohibiting the mailing of some publications.[23]

Note that during World War II, the FBI was authorized to use virtually any method to track down and conduct surveillance on foreign nationals and American citizens, even if they were only, in Attorney General Robert Jackson's words, "encouraging opposing ideologies." Naturalized citizens could have their citizenship taken away and be deported, and many were.

Internment and Other Restrictions on Travel

During World War II, 25,655 non-citizens living in the United States were interned or deported because of their ethnicity or nationality, rather than their words or conduct, including 11,229 Japanese, 10,905 Germans, 3,278 Italians, 52 Hungarians, 25 Romanians, 5 Bulgarians, and 161 other foreign nationals living in the United States.[24] For such people, the Supreme Court held, in Johnson v. Eisentrager (1950), that

> executive power over enemy aliens, undelayed and unhampered by litigation, has been deemed, throughout our history, essential to wartime security. This is in keeping with the practice of the most enlightened of nations and has resulted in treatment of alien enemies more considerate than that which has prevailed among any of our enemies and some of our allies. This statute was enacted or suffered to continue by men who helped found the Republic and formulate the Bill of Rights, and although it obviously denies enemy aliens the constitutional immunities of citizens, it seems not then to have been supposed that a nation's obligations to its foes could ever be put on a parity with those of its defenders. The resident enemy alien is constitutionally subject to summary arrest, internment and deportation whenever a "declared war" exists.[25]

So the power to intern or deport comes into effect only when war has been declared. Today we are under attack not by a nation but by groups of individuals. Yet for the first time in human history, the destructive power of terrorists can be as great as that of a traditional nation-state that has declared war. We need a mechanism to deal with this change.

But for the moment, I want to focus on the reasoning of our law during World War II. The country was then faced with the prospect of large numbers of people—identifiable by ethnicity, not conduct—who were real or potential enemies. The logic of the Supreme Court's opinion in *Johnson* v. *Eisentrager* is applicable to the situation we face today.[26] The Court held that people ethnically connected to the war-makers are more likely to support them than are others—and our country at war has a right to protect itself from this presumed higher risk of danger. This is true regardless of the personal innocence of particular individuals. The term we would use today is "ethnic profiling," and two hundred years of American law and practice during wartime permits ethnic profiling for the common defense.

We can only guess how President Roosevelt, Justice Felix Frankfurter, General George Marshall, California attorney general Earl Warren, and our other wartime leaders would have dealt with our national security dilemmas today. Would they have shrugged their shoulders and accepted that the latest trends in law meant they couldn't protect America from mortal danger? Would they have let the enemy win and America perish?

To even ask these questions is to answer no, because every time those leaders faced a legal challenge to protecting America during wartime, they found a way to overcome it. Our leaders during World War II planned to win the war, not come up with gentlemanly excuses for losing it.

President Roosevelt, California attorney general Warren, and the U.S. Supreme Court proved this with the internment of American citizens of Japanese ancestry after Pearl Harbor. By far the most comprehensive, up-to-date, and incisive analysis of these internments is Michelle Malkin's book *In Defense of Internment*, published in 2004. Her book is essential reading for a full understanding of the historical facts.

For my purposes here, I merely want to review the Supreme Court's legal reasoning in upholding internment (as well as curfews and other conditions) in the case of individual American citizens against whom there was no evidence of personal transgression. The Court justified the decision under the principle of military necessity. Chief Justice Harlan Fiske Stone, writing the majority opinion, first approvingly quoted the words of former chief justice Charles Evans Hughes: "The war power of the national government is the power to wage war successfully. [And it is] not for any court to sit in review of the wisdom of the actions of the Executive or of Congress, or to substitute its judgment for theirs. If the Court could say there was a rational basis for the military decision, it would be sustained."[27]

Chief Justice Stone went on to explain in the majority opinion that the war power

> extends to every matter and activity so related to war as sub-stantially to affect its conduct and progress. The power is not restricted to the winning of victories in the field and the repulse of enemy forces. It embraces every phase of the national defense, including the protection of war materials and the members of the armed forces from injury and from dangers which attend the rise, prosecution and progress of war.[28]

The Court specifically rejected the argument that if a curfew were necessary, every American citizen, not just those of Japanese ancestry, should have to comply. The Court responded that it was not necessary to "inflict obviously needless hardship on the many."

Compare that reasoning to our current practice in airport searches since September 11, where our government's policy is precisely to impose obviously needless hardship on the many, when they search eighty-year-old grandmothers equally with, or instead of, twenty-three-year-old Arab men.

The Court concluded with the comprehensive assertion:

> Whatever views we may entertain regarding the loyalty to this country of the citizens of Japanese ancestry, we cannot reject as unfounded the judgment of the military authorities and of Congress that there were disloyal members of that population, whose number and strength could not be precisely and quickly ascertained. We cannot say that the war-making branches of the Government did not have ground for believing that in a critical hour such persons could not readily be isolated and separately dealt with, and constitute a menace to the national defense and safety, which demanded that prompt and adequate measures be taken to guard against it.[29]

In essence, the Court found that if there was any rational support for discriminating on the basis of race, such discrimination was justified under the circumstances of a war menace. Of course, these opinions were written years before the Court ruled in *Brown* v. *Board of Education* that any discrimination on the basis of race was "suspect" and could be justified only with "extraordinarily strong" reasons.[30]

The *Brown* decision was right to hold racial discrimination to the toughest possible justification. It is the founding document of our noble effort to gain a truly color-blind country. But in that case and all that have followed it, the issue of racial discrimination did not arise in the context of war powers necessary for the United States to survive a mortal danger.

A decent man makes different judgments in different circumstances. This point is literally true in the twin cases of Japanese internment and *Brown* v. *Board of Education*. It was Earl Warren, California attorney general in 1942, who called for the internment of Americans of Japanese ancestry, and it was Earl Warren, chief justice of the Supreme Court in 1954, who outlawed racial segregation in the public schools. It is a good guess that if the issue of race-based discrimination had been considered a national defense necessity in 1954, Justice Warren would have decided as he had in 1942.

Restrictions on Free Speech

Since the Civil War, presidents have had the power to prosecute American citizens and residents for advocating America's defeat during wartime, under charges of sedition or espionage. During World War I, people could be prosecuted—and thousands were—for making disloyal, scurrilous, or abusive comments about the government; for saying anything to bring the armed forces into contempt, scorn, or disrepute; or for favoring the cause of any country with which the United States was at war.31 There were more than two thousand prosecutions and a thousand convictions for sedition during World War I.32 Even greater numbers were prosecuted and imprisoned during the Civil War; perhaps as many as thirty thousand people were imprisoned for sedition from 1861 to 1865.33

During World War II, however, whether people were intimidated by the history of sedition prosecutions or whether there was simply less sedition occurring, there were actually fewer prosecutions, a little over two hundred in all. Among them were members of fascist and socialist organizations, as well as, interestingly, black Muslims who identified themselves with the Japanese rather than the United States. But most important from a legal point of view were members of the Jehovah's Witnesses who were prosecuted for refusing to let their children recite the Pledge of Allegiance.

Liberal Supreme Court justice Felix Frankfurter wrote the majority opinion in the case regarding the Jehovah's Witnesses. He upheld the school expulsions and parental prosecutions for violating compulsory attendance laws and gave a shrewd explanation for the right of government to sometimes override the rights of religion, dissent, and conscience: "But to affirm that the freedom to follow conscience has itself no limits in the life of society would deny that very plurality of principles which, as a matter of history, underlies protection of religious toleration."[34]

Justice Frankfurter also observed that "the mere possession of religious convictions which contradict the relevant concerns of a political society does not relieve the citizen from the discharge of political responsibilities. The necessity for this adjustment has again and again been recognized."[35] This is particularly applicable to the situation we face today as radical Islamists are demanding to be covered by sharia rather than by their nation's laws.

Although Justice Frankfurter is remembered in history as a great liberal, in the 1940s liberalism still understood our country's history and government's role in unifying our nation. Precisely on that point, Justice Frankfurter wrote:

> The question remains whether school children, like the Gobitis children, must be excused from conduct required of all the other children in the promotion of national cohesion. We are

dealing with an interest inferior to none in the hierarchy of legal values. National unity is the basis of national security. To deny the legislature the right to select appropriate means for its attainment presents a totally different order of problem from that of the propriety of subordinating the possible ugliness of littered streets to the free expression of opinion through distributing handbills.[36]

Frankfurter raised the issue of the mandatory Pledge of Allegiance to an even higher level when he wrote, "Situations like the present are phases of the profoundest problem confronting a democracy, the problem which Lincoln cast in the memorable dilemma: 'Must a government of necessity be too strong for the liberties of its people, or too weak to maintain its own existence?' "[37]

I have quoted Justice Frankfurter at some length because his words highlight how dangerously abstract and ahistorical our thinking has become in the last few decades. Rooseveltian liberalism, whatever one may think of its economic nostrums, was in the practical business of defending the nation. Today, schoolchildren, senators, and elite journalists—and probably even most Americans—would giggle at the idea of applying Frankfurter's lofty words to the defense of the modest little Pledge of Allegiance.

But back then, as now, we were a nation of newly arrived immigrants, threatened from abroad and bombarded with destructive ideologies. Then, it was Communism and Fascism. Today, it is multiculturalism, political correctness, and among the Muslim population, radical Islam. American liberals in the 1940s had seen how Nazism had corrupted a great, civilized population in Germany in the 1920s and 1930s, how the Weimar government of Germany had lost control of the political culture, and as a result, how national unity had dissolved.

When Justice Frankfurter wrote "national unity is the basis of national security," this was no mere abstract idea. He was living in an age when many once great nations were divided, defeatist, and vulnerable to conquest. *Ft. Minersville School Dist.* v. *Gobitis* was argued on April 25, 1940. He delivered his opinion on the Pledge of Allegiance on June 3, 1940. On May 10, 1940, Germany had invaded France. On May 14, Holland had surrendered to Germany. On May 26, Britons had begun the evacuation of all their troops and as many French soldiers as they could take, 338,000 troops in all, from the beaches of Dunkirk. France was in complete disarray, with organized French military opposition crumbling in the face of the Nazi onslaught. The inevitable happened, and France surrendered on June 22.

A divided and defeatist France had been conquered by a barbaric, but again united, Germany. Britain appeared to be next, desperately evacuating the continent of Europe, leaving the heavy guns, trucks, and equipment on the beaches of Dunkirk. These were the headlines Justice Frankfurter would have been reading over breakfast as he thought about the need for a pledge of allegiance. No wonder he wrote that "national unity is the basis of national security." He almost certainly remembered the famous vote at Oxford University in the 1930s, when a pacifist majority of the elite British male students announced that they "would not fight for King or country."

To read Justice Frankfurter's opinions, and those of many other Supreme Court justices in the late 1930s and 1940s, is to see the work of superbly educated, highly civilized, freedom-loving men who knew American history and had thought deeply about preserving the nation.

Evil was on the march. It was overwhelmingly powerful, well organized, and pitiless. All around the world, from Singapore to Norway, civilization was being routed by the evil mass forces of Nazi Germany and its ally Japan, while Soviet Communism was corrupting minds in democracies from France to America to China. In those days, when Supreme Court justices—liberal, moderate, and conservative—sat down to write opinions, they knew their words and findings mattered. Wrongly decided cases wouldn't merely expose the justices to rude comments in fashionable newspapers and magazines. Wrongly decided cases might expose the United States to disunity, sabotage, revolution, or conquest.

Under such circumstances, they were more than prepared to let Congress give the president of the United States broad powers to defend our country, and they were unlikely to interfere with the president carrying out such powers or to second-guess the military's decisions. The Court would draw lines and preserve the essence of our freedoms, but the justices were practical men who understood that the broadest enforcement of every last theoretical right and privilege might well be purchased at the price of losing our most basic right: the right to effectively defend ourselves.

The Smith Act, passed in 1940, outlawed sedition, making it a crime to knowingly advocate, abet, advise, or teach the duty, necessity, desirability, or propriety of overthrowing the United States government by violence, or to affiliate with an association that did so. The most famous prosecution under that law came in 1948, after the Nazis had been defeated but just as the well-justified fear of Communism was arising. Twenty-one members of the central committee of the U.S. Communist Party were indicted, and twenty of them were convicted. In a subsequent case, 131 Communists were charged under the Smith Act, and barely more than a dozen escaped conviction.[38]

The Supreme Court upheld the constitutionality of the Smith Act in the case of *Dennis v. United States.* I want to quote a few lines from that ruling, because they are so sensible—and were so obviously sensible sixty years ago—yet would probably be judged shocking by most commentators and news outlets today. In ruling that a defendant could be convicted and sent to prison for advocating the violent overthrow of our government—even though he had never acted on that advocacy, never bought a gun or a bomb, never organized an act of violence—Justice Frankfurter, in a concurring opinion, wrote, "It is not forbidden to put down force and violence, it is not forbidden to punish its teaching or advocacy, and the end being punishable, there is no doubt of the power to punish conspiracy for the purpose."

Chief Justice Frederick Moore Vinson held, "Overthrow of the Government by force and violence is certainly a substantial enough interest for the Government to limit speech: indeed, this is the ultimate value of any society, for if a society cannot protect its very structure from armed internal attack, it must follow that no subordinate value can be protected."[39]

In giving practical meaning to the "clear and present danger" test, the circumstance that triggers the right of the government to proscribe speech, the court endorsed the succinct and logical test crafted by Judge Learned Hand in the lower court in the *Dennis* case: "In each case [courts] must ask whether the gravity of the 'evil,' discounted by its improbability, justifies such invasion of free speech as is necessary to avoid the danger."

These are the words of principled jurists who were aware of the human history that gave them the power to make such rulings and were alive to the practical means by which any freedom could be maintained in a world filled with evil and violent forces. They were unwilling to dismiss as harmless any expression of intent to destroy by violence the nation and constitution they had taken an oath to protect.

These men, and in fact most Americans sixty years ago, did not suffer from a fetishistic idolatry of any absolute "rights." They mentally labored throughout their productive judicial lives to find a practical balance between the seeming dilemma of enjoying our rights in the present while also permitting government actions designed to protect our rights in the future.

They lived in an America that, though powerful and confident in itself, had not yet become the massive, nuclear-armed, sole superpower of the late twentieth and early twenty-first centuries. They lived at a time when even FDR's government could not do everything for the people. Infectious disease was still rampant. Stark poverty was still prevalent throughout much of the country. Many, perhaps most, people could not afford top-rate medical treatment—and the government had not yet stepped in with Medicare and Medicaid. Even state-of-the-art medical science in 1945 could not protect a millionaire from many of the medical threats to life that the government protects the pauper from today.

In short, Americans were strong and confident, but did not feel invulnerable, either individually or as a nation. America was not yet the colossus of the world. And this sense of vulnerability to danger shaped the Supreme Court's interpretation of government powers—particularly in times of war. It also shaped public opinion. No wave of popular outrage was expressed at any of these court opinions. Some left-wing intellectuals and journalists opposed the decisions, but the logic of the times had driven the decisions, and the public was in tune with that logic.

Free speech, cherished as it had been since before our founding, was seen to have practical limits when the nation was threatened in war. Children could be compelled to pledge their allegiance, even if their religion forbade it, because national security required national unity. Americans were determined to teach their children to be loyal to

America, for fear that disunity would yield national insecurity and, perhaps, national defeat.

And while Americans continued to be free to say almost anything they wanted, even during war, if they spoke in favor of violence against the government or of violently overthrowing the government, the American public and the Supreme Court were perfectly prepared to put them in prison.

Today, on the Internet as well as on our best college campuses, people—even professors—are speaking in ways that could have landed them in federal prison sixty years ago. But the logic of our time is to ignore such "harmless" conduct. Even in the face of the Islamist terrorist threat, we are not united in self-defense. Our government makes little effort to encourage such unity of purpose. There is little public clamor to bring all our national powers to bear on behalf of such unity and vigilance.

We are the colossus of the world. We spend billions of dollars each year on potato chips and hairspray. We have a volunteer army to fight our wars. That seems to be enough. The Homeland Security Department keeps crying wolf about yellow and orange terrorist alerts. Stop scaring us, we say, it must be a ploy. Let the government protect us, but not intrude on our lives. Keep track of the terrorists, but don't even glance at me.

Perhaps we have the luxury of such profligate indifference. History will reveal the answer. But history has a tendency to judge harshly those nations or peoples who are indifferent to their own protection. Half-hearted efforts, misdirected priorities, and unnecessary vulnerabilities are not the hallmarks of nations that survive adversity. They are more likely to be the themes of lamentations for lost glories sung by the survivors of defeated and ruined cultures. You can hear their sorrowful tunes among what is left of the Celtic peoples who long ago were over-whelmed by Germanic tribes in Britain. You can hear them in the songs and chants of American Indians on the paltry reservations, which is all that is left of their once proud patrimony, after the Europeans came to the Americas. Still proud, it is true, but more sad than proud.

Once upon a time in America, we were a nation that would not take any such chances. Once upon a time, we worried a little less about the rights that we possessed, and worried a little more about the wrongs our enemies might imminently inflict upon us. Once upon a time, we were stripped for action and saved the world. During World War II, we did what was necessary to win the war—and in so doing, we preserved our rights.

CHAPTER SEVEN

A World in Transition

G EORGE ORWELL PUT IT WELL, writing in 1940, "I thought of a rather cruel trick I once played on a wasp. He was sucking jam on my plate, and I cut him in half. He paid no attention, merely went on with his meal, while a tiny stream of jam trickled out of his severed esophagus. Only when he tried to fly away did he grasp the dreadful thing that had happened to him. It is the same with modern man. The thing that has been cut away is his soul, and there was a period—twenty years, perhaps—during which he did not notice."[1] In Orwell's view, Western man lost his soul in the aftermath of World War I.

In 1914, most people in Britain—even informed people—did not see that world war and catastrophe were coming until it was too late. When British prime minister Herbert Asquith opened his Cabinet meeting on July 24, 1914, just ten days before Britain declared war in what would become World War I, the possibility of war had not even been discussed. In fact, foreign policy of any type had not come up in over a month. Even the assassination of the heir to the Austro-Hungarian throne, Archduke Ferdinand, and his consort, Sophie, in

Sarajevo on June 28 had not required Cabinet discussion. "Indeed, in all the capitals of Europe, the reaction to the assassination . . . was calm to the point of indifference."[2] The British Cabinet discussed, as it did so often, not foreign affairs, but the Irish question. A young Winston Churchill, then first lord of the admiralty, described how that meeting ended:

> The discussion had reached its inconclusive end, and the Cabinet was about to separate, when the quiet grave tones of Sir Edward Grey's voice were heard reading a document which had just been brought to him from the Foreign Office. It was the Austrian note to Serbia. He had been reading or speaking for several minutes before I could disengage my mind from the tedious and bewildering debate which had just closed. . . . The note was clearly an ultimatum. . . . The parishes of Fermanagh and Tyrone faded back into the mists and squalls of Ireland, and a strange light began . . . to fall upon the map of Europe.

After the meeting, both Churchill and Prime Minister Asquith wrote private notes indicating that while war might break out on the continent, it wouldn't affect Britain. Asquith wrote, "Happily, there seems to be no reason why we should be anything more than spectators." Churchill prepared to join his family at the beach for their end of summer holiday.[3]

Ten days later, Britain declared war on Germany, leading to the death of 750,000 British troops, ten million military deaths for all the combatant nations, and the fall of three of the four great European dynasties: the Romanov in Russia, the Hohenzollern in Germany, and the Habsburg in Austria. World War I led to the end of a European way of life and the rise of Lenin, Stalin, Hitler, and the immeasurable butcheries that made the twentieth century man's bloodiest—so far.

It all seems so obvious now, what was waiting for Britain and Europe in the last weeks of July 1914 while Winston Churchill, often so prescient, was happily preparing for a beach holiday. But as Danish philosopher and theologian Søren Kierkegaard once observed, life must be lived forward, but can only be understood backwards; so, too, history. While we are sometimes able to anticipate and prepare for great changes in history, it is more often the case that leaders of great nations—both the shrewd and the ordinary—fail to notice a major historical discontinuity until it has burst into universal awareness.

In 1789, as the Bastille was being stormed in Paris, King Louis XVI asked the Duke de la Rochefoucauld, "Is this a rebellion?" The duke responded, "No, Sire, it is a revolution." Right up until the revolution, and beyond, the king of France could not sense the great historic discontinuity that was about to transform the world and sweep away his monarchy.

In another moment when the hinges of history were swinging, an American president couldn't imagine that he had the power to stop it. In February 1861, seven Southern states had left the Union. President James Buchanan denounced the secession but maintained that he had "no authority to decide what shall be the relation between the federal government and South Carolina," which was the first state to secede.[4] A month later, the new president, Abraham Lincoln, found this authority and fought the Civil War to save the nation.

It has not been only recently that sudden and historic discontinuities have fallen upon peoples. Consider briefly the shocking shift of European life between the thirteenth and fourteenth centuries. The thirteenth century experienced warm weather; bountiful crops; a population that expanded to over seventy-three million people; the high point of cathedral building; the founding of the universities; the flowering of science, theology, mathematics, and literature; and the works of Dante, Roger Bacon, Saint Thomas Aquinas, Saint Francis of Assisi, Marco Polo,

Albertus Magnus, Petrus Peregrinus, and William of Occam, among so many others. Economic growth and expansion through the founding of the Hanseatic League and other forces funded the flowering of Europe's High Middle Ages.

Then the fourteenth century brought climate change (in the form of a mini Ice Age); depressed harvests; the Hundred Years' War between England and France; and the Black Death, which cut Europe's population by 40 percent, to about forty-five million. Whole villages became ghost towns. Laborers, suddenly in short supply, improved their bargaining position against the landed class. The Catholic Church, too, was rocked by dissent, and the social and cultural stability of Europe was undermined. Then, within decades, Europe rejuvenated itself once again and exploded into its Renaissance and age of discovery.

It is the conceit of people living in almost every successful age to presume that their nation or civilization has finally mastered the vagaries of life and history; even great minds can come to believe that they have arrived at the end of history. But the inevitable, if lamentable, truth is that moments of supreme success and confidence are really just history catching her breath before again instructing the next batch of students on the eternal truth: *Sic transit gloria mundi*: "So passes away the glory of the World," Thomas à Kempis's reminder in *De Imitatione Christi* of the transitory nature of human vanities.

Today, both Europe and America tend to see the rise of terrorism as a challenge to be managed within the larger context of current politics. While the United States under President George W. Bush has partly reorganized the government's internal security and intelligence services, given a few more investigative tools to law enforcement agencies through the Patriot Act, and slightly increased its defense spending, there has been no transformational change in American politics. In

Europe, there has been no significant modification at all of internal security procedures, intelligence reform, or defense spending.

It is true that America and a few of its allies acted promptly after September 11, 2001. The United States, under President Bush's admirable leadership, swiftly removed the Taliban from Afghanistan, overturned Saddam Hussein's regime in Iraq, induced the government of Pakistan to switch most of its loyalties from the terrorists to the West, and reversed a half-century of American policy that supported dictators and kings in the Middle East for the sake of stability. President Bush's insistent push for democracy in the Middle East and elsewhere is a genuinely radical departure from the status quo, and must, in fairness, be judged a major discontinuity in American foreign policy, whatever its eventual results. But most U.S. government policy, particularly domestic policy, remains much the same, as does the policy of the EU states. Most critically, our strategic thinking and our sense of our place in history remain little changed.

Yet if my assessment of the future is right, the West is inexorably moving into a time that will be very different economically, culturally, and politically from what we've experienced since the end of World War II. How jarring this discontinuity will be, and whether we will prevail during this next period of our history, will depend on how—and how soon—our leaders and the public recognize the magnitude of the change and react to it.

The history of a nation, a people, or a civilization is not linear; nor is it a predictable cycle in the sense that a nation arises, becomes vigorous and develops its classic form, then succumbs to excess, then decadence, and finally death. Such intellectual constructs are too neat. They are often also historically contradicted. China has repeatedly emerged from decadence back to youthful vigor, as she is doing currently. Britain went from the licentiousness of the Shakespearean era (late sixteenth century), to the moral rectitude of Cromwellian England (mid-seventeenth century), to the frivolity of the Restoration (mid- to late seventeenth century), to a period of evangelical and Methodist moral revival (late eighteenth century), to the self-conscious moral rectitude of the Victorian era (nineteenth century), which itself gave way to Edwardian extravagance (early twentieth century). The United States has gone through such changes as well, from the mid-eighteenth-century Great Awakening, to the self-indulgent and individualistic 1920s and 1960s, to the periods of self-sacrifice in the 1860s and 1940s.

The powerful image of the Roman Empire falling from vigor to decadence to oblivion continues to capture the minds of theoreticians of civilizational rises and falls. But grand theories of predictable change usually assume that current trends will continue, while in real life we are constantly surprised at the amount of change we have experienced, even when the change comes steadily over several decades. In fact, nothing seems more improbable to most of us than our own impending old age and death. Despite knowing that such events are inevitable, we find it startling that the adult just gaining his or her stride in life is an impending senior citizen.

Even in a country as oriented to change as America, we have a deep psychological need to see stability. After World War I, President Warren Harding promised a "return to normalcy." Well, if he meant peace, he was right. But 1920s America would hardly have been considered normal by the measure of pre–World War I America.

Historians now see the 1920s as the beginning of modern times: revealing clothes for women; the birth of the age of celebrity; wild independence from previous, strictly enforced modest behavior; the average man or woman buying stocks in the stock market; fantastic prosperity; mass consumerism, mass communications, and exciting inventions constantly emerging, including radios, the movies, and automobiles. And, of course, as soon as the 1920s lifestyle had become the norm, no one could imagine the party ever ending—until the stock market crash of 1929 heralded the Great Depression.

ECONOMIC WAR

Similar discontinuities are likely to happen today, including in the economies of the West. Remember that one of Osama bin Laden's primary goals is to destroy our economy. There are manifest trends that could make his plan of economic warfare a painful reality.

Since the end of World War II, the West has experienced sixty years of general political stability and economic prosperity based on international trade. The two obvious counter-forces are the spread of jihadist Islam and the West's impending fiscal and demographic social welfare crises. These counter-forces could impose major cultural, economic, and national security discontinuities on the West.

Europe's social welfare crisis is even more severe than ours, because of the greater generosity of its social welfare systems, the lower productivity of European economies, and Europe's severe aging crisis, due to low birthrates. In Europe and the United States, the central fact is that the boomer generation has voted itself more health and retirement benefits than the following generations are likely to be able or willing to pay.

The fiscal impact of this crisis has obvious economic, political, and cultural implications that will affect our national security and our way of life. Almost certainly, social welfare benefits will have to be adjusted downward, probably quite dramatically. The Germans are already beginning to work through the politics of that challenge. The United States has not yet even begun to conceptualize how it would pay for full health care coverage for retirees. Medicare spending alone, currently about 2 percent of the nation's GDP, is on a trend line to rise to 14 percent by the 2050s. Medicare and Social Security spending together would equal 20 percent of the entire economy and more than 100 percent of that future federal budget. The unfunded liability of Medicare is $61 trillion, according to the Medicare trustees.[5] Medicaid budgets for the poor are not even included in such numbers, although millions of boomers will be expecting such aid for their nursing home days.

These are trends that cannot continue, but as of this writing, there is insufficient political will in the United States to even rationally adjust the lesser problem of Social Security under-funding. We are living on the cusp of a substantial economic discontinuity with potentially enormous consequences: from the inevitable financial and medical insecurities of a generation that has not saved sufficiently for its retirement, to the rationing of health care, to the possible encouragement of euthanasia as a means of cutting costs for sick patient and elderly care.

With a little bad luck in the future, things could be worse yet. Anti-globalization activists are already applying political pressure to curtail the international trading system that has yielded our unprecedented prosperity. As the low wage/high productivity economies of China and India—with their two and a half billion people—put further pressure on the international trade regime, the chance of curtailed international trade (and thus reduced prosperity) increases. To protect American workers from Chinese-level wage rates, there will be increasing pressure to build tariff and quota walls. While such actions will put a floor under the wage slide and maintain adequate economic activity, the

American economy will be decidedly less prosperous than it could be with vibrant world trade.

Even if there were no terrorism threat, domestic political pressure in the United States (and elsewhere) is inexorably increasing for protectionist laws. Every year it gets harder to pass free trade bills through Congress. This year, an innocuous little trade bill for Central America is facing disproportionately powerful and emotional opposition. Many formerly strong free-trade advocates in Congress have quieted their public support, while other members are increasingly pro-protectionist. A recent chairman of the Republican Party told me that protectionist sentiment was rising to the point that he was deeply concerned about its implications for free trade.[6]

Other factors such as inflation, the effects of trade and budget deficits, and financial market dysfunctions could further slow growth and expose the economy to either sudden or sustained economic contractions. If such a recession hits (driving down the value of IRA stock portfolios and real estate) boomers might be trying to retire in an economic crisis approaching the magnitude of the Great Depression. They will be trying to unload their homes when there is a glut of real estate on the market, because the buyers for these homes will come from the smaller post-boomer generation; their equities will have to be sold at fire-sale prices; and Social Security payments, if not reformed, will be less than 75 percent of their current value.

But fiscal and demographic factors and rising protectionist agitation are not the only threat to our prosperity. Future terrorist attacks on airliners, shipping, or across America's borders with Mexico and Canada could have a similar restricting impact on trade. While the cost of sealing our borders with security would be high, the lost and slowed trade would be vastly more damaging to our economy.

Eventually it will dawn on Western leaders and public opinion that it would be safer to keep some distance between the West and Islam. Everything from Internet connections to immigration, to tourism, to business, to trade will be more carefully controlled, if not partially disconnected. Each restraint on the free flow of people, material, and words will act to marginally damage our economies.

Globalization expert Martin Wolf, associate editor and chief economics commentator at the London *Financial Times*, has calculated that the economic benefits we have enjoyed come from the relatively open world trade that has existed since 1945. He estimates that "U.S. incomes are $1 trillion per year higher due to the . . . country's increased integration with the world economy since 1945."[7] That amounts to almost 10 percent of GDP, or $10,000 per household per year.

If such open trade were interrupted, it could mean that the net assets for the average American family might be reduced by more than $200,000 over the next twenty years. As most Americans do not have $200,000 in net assets, they would be left with virtually no net assets. Even if the lost wealth is only half that figure, boomers are likely to live in a straitened retirement. And keep in mind that the government's take of total wealth is likely to go up as it struggles to keep a safety net under the public, as military costs of the war on terrorism go up, and as the massive costs of repairing and compensating after terrorist attacks go up.

It was only after World War II that a large, affluent, and reasonably economically secure middle class became the norm for Americans. (Prewar America was largely working-class and less economically secure.) If the benefits of globalized trade are substantially removed from our economy, we should expect that the period from 1914 to 1945 will provide a better guide to our future than 1945 to 2001.

Keep in mind that the world prior to World War I was almost as globalized and interconnected as it is today. It took a full eight decades to regain the level of world trade and connectedness that was lost when the world was pulled into the first great disaster of the twentieth century. The logic of the terrorist threat would drive us back into a more disconnected world. The level of disconnectedness and concomitant economic contraction in the near future are not knowable, of course, but we are only one or two major terrorist acts in the West away from finding out. Given the religious, economic, political, military, and cultural forces currently in turmoil, it would be improvident to base one's future on the assumption that current prosperous trends will continue indefinitely.

The boomer generation, born to prosperity, a sense of unending entitlement, and a highly developed sense of individual prerogatives and rights, has a substantial chance of facing its final decades in both economically and philosophically impoverished circumstances.

The best alternative is for the fabled (if often despised) boomer generation to directly face up to these challenges in order to defeat the jihadists, reform the welfare state, and put more emphasis on duty than on rights, and on the needs of the nation than on the desires of the individual. It will be ironic, but quite possible, that the Dionysian, profligate, demanding, self-centered boomer generation will end its days leading the nation to the necessary habits of self-denial, individual material restraint, giving rather than taking, and supporting a sense of collective national purpose.

These were the sentiments and values that the Depression and World War II engendered in the freedom-loving Americans of the boomers' parent generation. When danger comes, collective strength becomes more attractive than individual prerogative. Catching spies or terrorists becomes more important than vindicating novel extensions of our basic rights. Investments in capital goods are favored over investing in individual wants and needs. Making sure our young troops are well equipped becomes more important than making sure that retirees are well settled.

In such events, strong leaders tend to emerge to demand sacrifice, which is willingly given by the same public that in safer times would scornfully have rejected such pleadings. In the mid-1930s, British prime minister Stanley Baldwin became vastly popular after his public brag that he wanted to spend money on housing, not armaments. By 1939, his memory was bitterly cursed by the same public who had only recently cheered him.

Older boomers will have to decide how much of their children's scarce resources they will fight to get their hands on, and how much can go toward the common purpose of our national defense and investment in productive assets. The cycle would seem to be completing itself, as it so often does in human history. Victory, delivered by stern values, yielded prosperity that permitted individualistic caprice, indulgence, overconfidence, excess, and a lack of vigilance that permitted danger to arise again and calls for stern values to overcome. As the boomers were present at the inception of the prosperity and safety cycle, so will they be present at the end of the cycle and the beginning of the danger-driven renewal.

IS DEMOGRAPHY DESTINY?

But there is one new element in both the anti-terrorist and economic threats: declining birthrates and eventually declining populations in Europe and, to a lesser extent, in the United States. Europe's capacity to make policy choices about how to fight terrorism and the Islamist threat will be substantially affected by how it understands its future population potentials. Birthrates, immigration, funding social welfare programs, future economic growth, and how to fight the War on Terror are all connected to population trends.

In 1972, Stanford University biologist Paul Ehrlich predicted that rapidly rising populations and dwindling food supplies meant that sixty-five million Americans would die of starvation by 1985. In actuality, not only did this not happen, but 61 percent of American adults are now judged to be overweight, according the U.S. surgeon general.[8] Ehrlich's book, *The Population Bomb*,[9] was, nonetheless, one of the most influential books of the last third of the twentieth century. It persuaded millions of Americans and Europeans that overpopulation was an imminent crisis and indirectly affected the population policies of Western governments and non-governmental organizations. Probably more than a few American and European women were inspired to choose not to have children to avoid "just adding to the problem."

In that book, Ehrlich projected what would happen if the doubling rate of the world population (thirty-five years, according to his calculations at the time) was projected out indefinitely. While he called that an "absurd" assumption, he went on at some length with a practical discussion of how we would manage such a situation. First he noted that in nine hundred years the population would be 60,000,000,000,000,000 (sixty million billion), which would be equal to one hundred people for each square yard of ground on the planet.

Then he went into detail how we would house all those people in "a continuous two-thousand-story building covering the entire planet." He concluded that section of his book with the very reasonable-sounding proposition that the world population could not exceed sixty million

billion (implying it could perhaps go that high) because of the "heat limits" of the atmosphere's capacity to absorb the heat these people and their
activities would be generating.[10]

In 1994, the United Nations published its *World Population Prospects*,
in which it projected that the world's population in 2050 would be 9.8
billion people. Two years later, in its "1996 revisions," the UN reesti-
mated the number at 9.4 billion. The UN's "1998 revisions" revised
the number down to 8.9 billion.[11] In a period of four years, the United
Nations adjusted its estimates downward by almost a billion people.

In human affairs, nothing is inevitable, other than death and taxes. In
few areas are "current trends" less predictable than in this kind of demographic projection. Of course, the existing number of fertile women in
a population places practical limits on the next generation's birth numbers in absolute terms. As with turning the direction of an ocean liner,
a human population change requires a long lead time. But the fertility
rate can change much faster than experts recently thought possible.

As one of America's leading demographers, Nicholas Eberstadt,
observed recently, "What course will world fertility trends take? There
is no way for predicting with much certainty. The UN Population
Division summarized the state of knowledge succinctly: 'There exists
no compelling and quantifiable theory of reproductive behavior in low
fertility societies.' The same might be said about reproductive behavior
in contemporary societies with higher levels of fertility. As a practical
matter, fertility prediction is a matter of educated guesswork."[12]

Though demographers can't know the future, the recent past is fairly
well understood. In 1900, the world population stood at about 1.65 billion. By 2000, it had more than quadrupled to 6 billion. That was the
fastest increase—both in rate and in absolute numbers—in recorded
history. While this general growth was going on, a new factor in pop-

ulation sizes and rates emerged: sustained and progressive reductions in family size due to deliberate birth control. This started in France about two centuries ago, then spread to the rest of Europe and North America, and, in recent decades, to almost the entire rest of the world.[13]

The replacement rate for a population is an average of 2.1 babies per woman. Western Europe is currently at approximately 1.4. Russia is at about 1.3. The United States is at 2.07—just under replacement level, but we have many young, mostly Hispanic, immigrants helping our population rates. The West is not reproducing itself, and below-replacement birthrates are fast becoming a worldwide fact.

Birthrates in the Caribbean and Asia have slipped below replacement level, with rates ranging from 1.8 in China to 1.3 or 1.4 in Japan and Hong Kong. The rates are falling fairly rapidly even in countries like Iran, Mexico, Bangladesh, and Turkey. In Muslim North Africa— including Algeria, Libya, and Morocco—the rate has dropped by half in the last thirty years, to 3.3. Tunisia and Lebanon are estimated to be barely at the 2.1 replacement level, as is Syria. Rates remain high in sub-Saharan Africa and in most of the non-African Arab Middle East; for example, the birthrate in Saudi Arabia is 5.8; in Yemen it is 7.6.[14]

As birthrates slip below the replacement rate, two things happen. First, the average age of the population goes up. This becomes particularly important for funding retirement benefits, with ever fewer working and tax-paying younger people supporting ever more non-working and benefit-collecting older people. It is also significant for the overall productivity of the entire country. There is no example in history of a nation becoming more prosperous when it doesn't have an expanding population.

It is for this reason that the U.S. Social Security Trustees' report predicts an average U.S. economic growth of below 2 percent by mid-century. As our population level is projected to flatten out in the second half of this century, with an ever-increasing percentage of people retired from productive economic activity, there will be fewer consumers to buy the goods and services our economy can produce. So even if per capita productivity goes up, the overall increase in wealth will be held back by the fact that we have fewer workers.

Of course, radical increases in productivity deriving from new technologies, such as nanogenetic information and other yet-to-be-developed capacities, may produce more wealth than we will lose from our shrinking workforce. But it would be imprudent to base our planning on such speculation.

The problem is more acute in Europe, of course, because Europeans face a declining (not merely a flat) population rate. Until recently, immigration was the proposed European solution to the population problem. In fact, the problem is doubly acute for Europe because it has relied on immigrants from Muslim countries. The European public and some European governments are beginning to recognize their Islamic populations as a threat to their peace and security. The United States relies primarily on Hispanic Christian immigrants who, while they have their own challenges of cultural integration, are not a source of terrorism or supportive of terrorism.

Even if fertility rates rise, Europe will need a massive immigration—and the United States will need substantial immigration—of workers to avoid the demographic-fiscal contradictions that threaten the West's prosperity. Resolving these contradictions will depend on our cultural sense of who we are and who we want to be in the future. For Europeans, particularly, these decisions, these cultural judgments, will determine their ability to protect themselves from both Islamist terrorism and the prospect of a cultural transformation of Europe into Eurabia.

ECONOMICS AND CULTURE

"We should encourage a positive attitude towards economic migrants. We should consider them not as threats but as possible resources." That assertion, posed a few months ago by Franco Frattini, EU justice, freedom, and security commissioner, catches the central conflict in the European mind regarding the role of Islam in Europe in this transitional year of 2005.15

Revolving around the seemingly innocuous bureaucratic issue of whether the EU or individual European governments should define immigration policies is a growing fight for the heart and culture of Europe. The Germans and Austrians, in particular, are demanding to write their own immigration laws. Tighter immigration laws were the opening issue in the British parliamentary elections this year. The EU is hoping for a draft EU-wide law by the end of the year.

Until recently, it was generally assumed that Europeans would continue to fill the gap caused by their declining birthrates with mostly Muslim immigrants. The EU projects that within twenty-five years, Europe's workforce will decline by twenty million workers, unless immigrants are let in to fill the gap.

Germany's new immigration law went into effect on January 1, 2005 (though it could be overridden if the EU approves a continent-wide law). It reflects the schizophrenic condition of German and European thinking. The new law is a compromise in two ways. At a purely economic level, it is a compromise between labor and management, with management wanting more or less unlimited immigration, while labor, with 12 percent unemployment, wants less labor competition—even though millions of unemployed Germans either aren't qualified for or don't want the unfilled jobs waiting for the Muslim immigrants.

It is also a compromise between German security and economic interests. German intelligence services gained the right to investigate immigrants more fully for terrorist connections, and the law makes it easier for foreigners suspected of terrorist links to be deported. When Commissioner Frattini argued that immigration shouldn't be seen as a threat, he tacitly recognized that the economic case for immigrants was not likely to carry a European argument. European cultural identity and security were now widespread concerns.[16]

In making his case for one EU-wide immigration law, Commissioner Frattini sounds strangely like President Bush in his controversial guest-worker proposals for Mexican immigrants. Warning of illegal Muslim immigrants slipping into Europe by boat from North Africa, landing in Italy or Spain, he said, "Without a unified European approach, we risk having an ever greater number of illegal immigrants. These people then can't be integrated, and stay on the margins of society."[17] But, of course, legalizing immigrants is no substitute for effectively controlling borders and screening out unwanted or dangerous immigrants. And even if Europe could control its borders, what would it do with the Muslim nation of Turkey?

In an evocative example of Europe in transition and conflicted over what to do with the Muslims, the EU voted in late 2004 to open accession talks with Turkey, even while public opinion was moving swiftly negative on the idea. In a September 2004 poll published by *Le Figaro* in France, the French were against Turkey entering the EU by a majority of 56 percent to 36 percent. Catching one aspect of the public mood, then French prime minister Jean-Pierre Raffarin said, "Do we want the river of Islam to enter the riverbed of secularism?" This revealing phrase was emblematic that for France, at least, secularism has taken on the cultural role of a religion, an article of faith that transcends material con-

cerns. This suggests that it has the same unifying and excluding func-
tions that religion often plays in the culture of a people. Indeed, the
absolutist degree of French secularism is similar in intensity, if not in sub-
stance, to the current fundamentalist trends in Islam and Protestantism,
and to a lesser extent, in Orthodox Judaism. It might not be unfair to
say that many of the French are secular fundamentalists. Similarly, Valéry
Giscard d'Estaing, the former French president and the architect of the
proposed EU constitution, said that Turkish membership would signal
"the end of the EU. [Turkey is] not a European country. [It has] a different culture, a different approach and a different way of life."[18]

On a related note, more than 80 percent of Germans associate Islam
with terrorism,[19] and 57 percent believe all immigration is bad for Germany.[20] In other words, Germany, like the rest of Europe, has the official
policy of allowing massive Muslim immigration to deal with its population shortfall and concomitant social welfare funding crisis, while, at
the same time, an overwhelming majority of Germans are against it. And
yet for Germany, Turkey, with a population of more than seventy million, remains the primary source of immigrants. This is a classic profile
of a major national policy in rapid and fundamental transition.

Not only is Europe changing its views on Muslim immigration, but
Turkey is also changing its sense of itself. I had a wonderful conversation with ninety-three-year-old Otto von Habsburg, one of the
founders of the modern movement to unify Europe and the last crown
prince of the Habsburg Dynasty.[21] He has, for seventy years, worked to
build up what is now the EU. He was offered, but declined, the presidency of Hungary and served in the EU parliament for twenty years,
from 1979 to 1999.

He recounted the story of his many trips to Turkey over the last sixty
years, when he, from time to time, visited Mustafa Kemal Atatürk's

mausoleum in Ankara. Atatürk, the founder of secular Turkish government after World War I, left instructions for his casket to point 180 degrees away from Mecca, to emphasize the secular nature of his new Turkey. But von Habsburg noticed that, over the years, the casket was slowly moved a few degrees. On his most recent trip, he saw that the casket was now pointing directly toward Mecca.[22] And, of course, the Turkish people recently voted their first religious party into power.

CHRISTIANITY AND EUROPEAN CULTURE

While the Islamic world is growing, and growing more radical and insurgent, has Europe become largely a continent of post-Christian secular atheists? Is it morally governed by relativism? Does it lack any sense of moral purpose other than a jejune and effete tolerance? Is it a purely materialistic culture? Is Europe so drained of cultural vitality that it is unwilling to reproduce itself? Will it surrender to aggressive Islam?

For centuries, the Christian faith and its embodiment in the Church formed, shaped, inspired, and governed Europe. But now the question on many minds is whether Europe will no longer be a Christian continent, but a predominantly Muslim launching pad for terrorist assaults on a still proudly Judeo-Christian America.

It is astonishing how quickly this characterization of Europe has taken hold of thoughtful opinion both in the United States and in Europe. The two great facts that have given rise to it are the substantial drop in Christian church attendance and the alarming drop in birthrates in Europe. In the mere five years since those facts were noticed, the characterization of Europe as a faithless, dying civilization has gone from a curiosity to a cliché. It might yet be an escapable fate, but a prolonged sense of fatalism could be self-fulfilling. If current cultural and religious trends continue, it will happen.

As I noted earlier, however, the phrase "if current trends continue" is one of the most misleading guides to the future, particularly when applied to human actions and decisions. Challenge and response, not continuity, describe the progress of human affairs. Of course, a delayed or ill-judged response can still lead to catastrophe. But it seems remarkably unlikely that current religious and cultural trends will continue much longer in Europe.

Even the current condition is not nearly as bleak as some suggest. While cultural matters are never fully quantifiable, by far the most comprehensive and trusted cultural survey of Europe is the European Values Study, an academic, continent-wide survey, the most recently completed series of which was held in 1999–2000. The prior benchmark surveys were taken in 1981 and 1990.[23]

The first interesting statistic rebuts the impression that Europeans have lost their sense of geographic place and nationhood and instead identify with an amorphous Europe. When asked what geographic group they identify with most closely, 49 percent said their city or town, 28 percent said their country, 13 percent said their province, and only 3 percent said "Europe."[24]

That 90 percent of Europeans profess loyalty to their city, province, or country while only 3 percent are loyal to the idea of Europe rather smashes the assumption that nationalism—or at least some form of patriotism—is dead in Europe. Nor, despite the assertions of the multiculturalists, is European nationalism to be feared. It was largely the energies generated by patriotic and nationalistic feelings since the Treaty of Westphalia in 1648 that provided the impetus for European expansion and dominance in the world. The continuing attraction of nationalism is perhaps why voting in European parliamentary elections is so low, and why there is so much public resistance to a European Union Constitution.

The next revealing measure of cultural attitudes is what the survey calls solidarity: the degree to which Europeans care about and want to do something for various categories of people in distress. Sixty-four percent of Europeans are concerned about the conditions of elderly Europeans, 59 percent are concerned about sick Europeans, but only 18 percent care about the conditions of immigrants in Europe.[25]

So when elite European journalists and government officials sneer about right-wing xenophobia, they are sneering at about 82 percent of the total European population. Both the European and American media constantly report on "anti-immigrant" groups like the National Front Party, led by Jean-Marie Le Pen in France, or the neo-Nazis in Germany, and try to portray anti-immigrant political movements as lingering on the fringe. But when fringe groups advocate a critical issue on which eight out of ten voters agree with them, it is a signal that either irresponsible fringe groups will soon do shockingly well in elections, or that the major parties will embrace the fringe parties' winning issue.

The former instance is exactly what happened in 2002, when Le Pen garnered 20 percent of the vote and forced Jacques Chirac into a runoff election for president of France. Le Pen's campaign focused on the issue of Muslim immigration.[26] Since then, mainline parties have begun following suit across Europe, and in Britain both the Conservative and the Labour parties have campaigned on anti-immigrant platforms.

Now we come to the explicit questions of faith and religion. Whatever Europeans are, they are not atheists. Only 5 percent of Europeans say they are atheists, with another 10 percent claiming to be agnostics. Even in France, the birthplace and pitiless paragon of secularism and atheism, only 15 percent of Frenchmen consider themselves atheists, and another 25 percent claim to be agnostics. That leaves a full 60 percent of the French who claim some spiritual or religious faith.[27]

According to the European Values Study and other reliable surveys, about 40 percent of Europeans believe in a personal God, compared to about 60 percent of Americans.[28] About 50 percent of Europeans say God—whether called personal or otherwise—is highly important in their lives, compared to about 80 percent of Americans.[29]

So Europe is far from being a continent of non-believers: About 85 percent of Europeans profess some spiritual adherence, 50 percent say God is highly important in their lives and 40 percent express a faith in a personal God. Given that Europe's populations are still nominally about 90 percent Christian, the majority of those professing faith in a personal God are professing faith in Christ. While Americans are measurably more religious, still at least a third of Europeans express general faith in Jesus, and a full 85 percent express spiritual beliefs. Europeans might not talk this way at cocktail parties, but this is what they tell the most respected market survey organizations.

However, the statistics that catch the most public attention are church attendance rates. It is in these statistics that Europe seems so dramatically more secular. Regular church attendance in America is well above 50 percent, while in Europe it is well below 20 percent, although the range of attendance is very wide. Poland and Malta can claim 80 percent regular attendance, Ireland and Italy above 40 percent, and the Netherlands about 25 percent. Britain, Germany, and France are in the mid- to lower teens.[30] I should add that a more recent Gallup survey in September 2004 shows British church attendance up to 24 percent, with Canada's at 37 percent (up from 20 percent, a remarkable 16 percent rise in five years) and America's at 56 percent.[31]

From the foregoing rattle of statistics, I draw three large inferences. First, Europeans are hardly the soulless materialists many people believe them to be. Second, European churches and preachers are doing a terrible job of capturing their fair share of the faithful. And third, the different histories of church/state relations in Europe and the United States go a long way to explain the difference in religious practice on the two continents.

It is hard in Europe and America to get an accurate picture of what people privately think about religion. I trust anonymous survey results over public utterances. On the topics of religion, sex, and money, in particular, people tend to be afraid to express unpopular thoughts. In Manhattan, for example, people sometimes whisper the fact that they are faithful Christians—and then only when they have picked up a signal from another that he or she is also that way. I suspect that in Mississippi, people do the same before confessing their lack of faith.

Given that in Europe, currently, people tend to sneer at those of faith—be they Christian, Jew, or Muslim—it is a fair guess that there are more privately faithful people than it would seem in daily conversation. Likewise, in many parts of America currently, being without faith is becoming scorned. So it is probably the case that Americans (at least in the publicly faithful parts of America, the "red" states and counties) publicly overstate their faith. This hypocrisy or fear factor probably narrows—but hardly closes—the American and European gap of faith.

It is also the case throughout history that people have been moved from indifference to curiosity, from doubt to faith, and from one faith to another. The historic reluctance of the Jewish faithful to proselytize might explain, in part, the small but persistent size of that great faith, just as the Mormon enthusiasm for reaching out doubtless explains the fast-growing number of their faithful.

In fact, virtually everywhere that Christianity has been vigorously proselytized it has grown. In 1900, there were about 10 million Christians in Africa, out of a total population of 100 million. After a century of Christian outreach, there are about 390 million Christians out of a total population of about 850 million, giving Christianity the edge over Islam by about 50 million souls.[32]

In Asia, excluding China, there are 2.5 million new net converts per year.[33] According to former *Time* magazine correspondent David Aikman, there are currently about eighty million Christians in China, moving toward 25 to 30 percent of the population in thirty years.[34]

So the failure of the Catholic Church and the Protestant denominations in Europe to remotely match their evangelizing efforts in Africa, America, South America, and more recently in Asia is doubtless a measurable factor in Europe's current level of Christian faithful.

Finally, the Christian mission in Europe has been made more difficult, ironically, by the fact that Christianity has been the official established religion throughout Europe until recently, and remains at least nominally the established religion in many European countries. In contrast to America, where religious denominations were forced to compete on an even level for adherents and were not affiliated with the government, in Europe the Christian Church inherited much of the public disapproval of civil governments over the centuries and developed lazy habits of evangelization.

Ever since the French Enlightenment focused its accusatory eye of reason on hereditary governments, their emerging capitalist economies, and the established Christian churches of the state, European Christianity has been operating at a disadvantage. The whole thrust and direction of European thought since the French Enlightenment has been to turn people away from the Church. The French Revolution ushered in a godless Europe that became the handmaiden of socialism.

The alleged role of Christianity in deadening the pain of capitalist oppression was forever immortalized in the truly beautiful words of Karl Marx: "Religion is the sigh of the oppressed creature, the heart of a heartless world, and the soul of soulless conditions. It is the opium of the people. The abolition of religion as the illusory happiness of the people is the demand for their real happiness. To call on them to give up their illusions about their conditions is to call on them to give up the conditions that require illusions. The criticism of religion is, therefore, in embryo, the criticism of that vale of tears of which religion is the halo."[35]

Karl Marx, as he does so often, brilliantly diagnoses the relationship of forces, but gets the underlying fundamentals exactly wrong: He argues that people seek religion to give them comfort from the pain caused by capitalism. Get rid of capitalism, enact socialism, and the pain will end; then the people won't need religion.

This idea became the central tenet of progressive thought in Europe (and elsewhere) for a century and a half, during which time most progressive, educated Europeans bought into Marx's proposition (whether they knew he was the author or not). Christianity's affiliation with reactionary monarchy and cruel capitalism gave it a bad odor. Smart, sophisticated people—or people who wanted to think of themselves as smart and sophisticated, and who does not?—said they were not taken in by the "old lies" of capitalism and Christianity.

But in 1989, with the fall of the Soviet Union, the contradiction inherent in Marx's system of analysis was revealed: It is socialism, not capitalism, that causes the greater pain for humanity. While this vindication of capitalism does not reestablish the legitimacy of Christianity in the eyes of Europeans, for the first time in 150 years Christianity is unyoked from its bondage to—and its Marxist role as dissembler and protector for—despised capitalism. Christianity can now begin again to be considered on its own merits.

Considering all these elements, it would seem reasonable to assess the current state of religious faith, and particularly Christian religious faith, in Europe to be at a historically low point, from which measurable recovery is more probable than not.

Three general propositions and some anecdotal evidence are at least suggestive of an upturn for Christianity in Europe. The first proposition is simply that virtually all human societies find a need for religion. While trends or fashions may affect the intensity and breadth of a religion's presence in a society, there is no example of a sustained, faithless society. Of course, that proposition doesn't preclude a European turn to paganism or other non-Christian spiritual practices, but it does suggest that sustained and expanded secularism is unlikely.

In fact, science is beginning to develop theories and some possible evidence for the idea that the human mind is hard-wired to believe in religion. Evolutionary biologist David Sloan Wilson, in his book *Darwin's Cathedral*, argues that religion and morality are biologically evolved adaptations that allow human societies to function more effectively as a single unit rather than as a mere collection of individuals.

Pascal Boyer, the Henry Luce Professor of Collective and Individual Memory at Washington University in St. Louis, theorizes, with some evidence, that human brains, by virtue of their evolutionary history, "share certain conceptual dispositions which in turn make concepts particularly easy to learn and transmit, and therefore very frequent in otherwise diverse human cultures."[36] Recently, the *Guardian*, a very secular British newspaper, ran a long article on the scientific discussion about whether religion is a biologically developed survival mechanism.[37] The very presence of a long article on the new science of religion in an aggressively secular newspaper may itself be evidence of a renewed interest.

Moreover, periods of danger or war usually heighten the human inclination to seek religious guidance. As Europe is increasingly threat-ened by radical Muslim populations, as the social welfare system fails and has to be reduced, as Europeans, as Marx would diagnose, begin to suffer, there might be a European religious revival.

REMEMBERING THE WASP

At the beginning of this chapter, I quoted George Orwell's recollections on cruelly cutting a wasp in half and watching it suck jam that streamed out of its severed body. So too, Western man has been content to suck on the sweetness of prosperity, measuring contentment by quantity of consumption. Happy to have plates of jam set before us, we have been oblivious to the world beyond our plate; we have become numbed into shallow contentment.

As the wasp was disconnected from his lower body, we have been disconnected from our soul and our culture. We have forgotten what makes us more than a wasp. But unlike the wasp, we have the capacity to reconnect with our soul and culture. The sharp knife of adversity threatens; challenge and response is the history of man. Islam has made the challenge, and the response is up to us.

For both Europe and the United States, our cultural instincts will determine our fate: They will define our politics, our economics, and our fighting strategy. The next two decades will probably be decisive. We have reached the West's last chance to reclaim its cultural essence and thereby sustain our civilization from the intruding vigor of Islam. The West needs to recover its fighting faith.

CHAPTER EIGHT

The Way Forward

I OPENED THIS BOOK WITH A FRIGHTENING scenario of a rising Eurabia. Here's another scenario. Imagine that during the first week in
December, Islamist terrorists release smallpox viruses in shopping centers in Oklahoma, Georgia, and Pennsylvania. At first, no one knows
we've been attacked, because symptoms can be latent for up to
seventy-two hours. But after a few days, dozens of very sick people
turn up at Oklahoma City Hospital. Their mysterious symptoms are
reported to the Centers for Disease Control in Atlanta, which con-
firms that these patients have smallpox.

The federal government quickly identifies the three epicenters in
Georgia, Pennsylvania, and Oklahoma. But because of the inevitable
delay between infection and the appearance of symptoms, the contagion has spread far beyond these states—which is inevitable in a modern, urban, mobile population like ours.

The news media have a constant supply of new, more terrible facts
about the spreading disease and runs video of panicked Americans:
traffic jams from people fleeing cities; fistfights and small riots near

inoculation centers, supermarkets, drugstores, and hardware stores; heartbreaking images of the diseased victims; and, of course, a constant flow of politicians giving the public the benefit of their wisdom.

From the media, you learn that on average, each infected person transmits the virus to ten other people. The government determines that about three thousand people were initially exposed. The known lethality rate is about 30 percent. Many who survive are blinded or horribly disfigured. Others die from secondary biological (as opposed to viral) infections that ooze out of each pox, sending toxins back into the skin and bloodstream.

Despite the televised scenes of panic, Americans as a whole behave surprisingly well under the circumstances. There are fewer than a dozen reported instances of reprisal attacks on American Muslims. There is no large-scale violence in any city. Americans are as orderly in public as could be hoped for. But of course, they do whatever they can to protect themselves and their families. As a result, many hospital workers—and even some doctors—fail to show up at hospital and temporary treatment centers set up by the Federal Emergency Management Agency and by state and local governments. Public transportation comes to a halt. People stay home—and with companies short-staffed, there are consumer shortages of all kinds.

The government gives first priority to inoculating emergency health care professionals and other essential workers, as well as to National Guard troops who might be needed to maintain order. This delays the distribution of inoculations to the general public.

From the first week in December until the middle of February—when the disease has largely run its course—three million Americans are infected, a million die, and hundreds of thousands are permanently disfigured or blinded. Because of the lockdown on America's roads and transportation systems, the economy essentially ceases to function for more than two months. An estimated $2 trillion of economic activity is lost. Regional supply shortages mean that some areas are virtually starving. Two-thirds of the million dead were either of working age or younger.

Now it is March. You have buried one of your children. Your best friend died, too, but his body was burned in a government-enforced mass disposal of corpses. Congress has reconvened for another round of emergency legislation, including the National Survival Act.

This terrorist scenario is not the product of my imagination. It comes from a test run named "Dark Winter," performed by the federal government in July 2001. The exercise was carried out at Andrews Air Force Base with the assistance of technical experts from Johns Hopkins University.[1]

Playing the part of the president was former Democratic senator Sam Nunn. Playing the part of the director of Central Intelligence was former CIA director James Woolsey. The actual progression of events was, of course, more detailed than my summary, but it showed that even if all levels of government—federal, state, and local—acted competently, they would still have been incapable of containing the disaster. One lesson learned from this study has been put into practice: We have developed millions of smallpox vaccines for emergency public use. But another important recommendation has not been implemented. President Bush asked all health workers to be vaccinated, but a large majority refused because of the small risks posed by the vaccine itself. The program was not mandatory.

Keep in mind, not only was this scenario plausible enough to justify a major federal government mock disaster test *before* September 11, but concern for an Islamist bioterrorist attack has also heightened considerably since then, to the point that the head of Interpol publicly announced that he thought it a "real" possibility that Europe would be subject to such an attack.

The head of Interpol, the top intra-European law enforcement coordinating agency, is obviously not in thrall to President Bush. Interpol executives might pay some political attention to the leaders of France and Germany, but those governments, and Europe in general, have tended to downplay the risks of Islamist terrorist attacks. So it is noteworthy that Interpol's assessment agreed with that of American and British anti-terrorism and law enforcement experts.

The consensus of terrorist experts is that Islamist terrorist organizations have access to biological, radiological, and chemical (and, of course, conventional) explosive devices; they have the potential to launch cyber-attacks; and they have thousands of trained terrorists. Hezbollah—the Lebanon-based terrorist organization backed by Iran and Syria—is judged to have the ability to launch even bigger worldwide terrorist operations than al Qaeda.

It is a subject of intense fear in both our government and others that Islamic militants might come into possession of a nuclear weapon. I reported in 2002 on *The McLaughlin Group* television show (and *Newsweek* confirmed the story a week later) that it was fear of a possible suitcase-type nuclear weapon that had kept Vice President Dick Cheney at least five miles away from the White House for an extended period of time. This was to ensure continuity of the government in case the White House was targeted with such a nuclear explosive.

Because four years have passed since the attack on the World Trade Center and the Pentagon, the fear-induced adrenaline level of the public has ebbed. But fear has some useful attributes, especially as a tool to focus our attention, and I worry that we are growing forgetful of the threat of another September 11. We have experienced this "forgetful-ness" before, when, after the oil embargoes of the 1970s, American pol-icy (and consumer demand) briefly shifted toward oil conservation and alternative fuels, only to revert to our first choice of big cars, big engines, and fossil fuels.

The difference is that if the government fails to remedy future energy supply threats, the price of gas goes up, but life goes on. With Islamic terrorism, the consequence of the same pattern of slovenly, for-getful government inaction could have a catastrophic price.

What follows is what I believe our government must do now.

DECLARE WAR

When President Bush declared war on terrorism, it did not, legally, put the country on a war footing (even if congressional authorizations for the Afghan and Iraq wars might be deemed the legal equivalent of a dec-laration of war). What we need is a clear congressional—as prescribed by the Constitution—declaration of war. Congress should declare war on the Islamist jihadists.

Up until now, we have never accurately named the enemy or the danger. If the government can't speak the real name and nature of the enemy, it becomes impossible to explain, or even design, a policy for victory. This is why President Bush—who has tried to talk around the problem of radical Islam—has seemed (to his critics) foolish or deceit-ful, neither of which he is.

Naming the Islamist jihadists as the formal enemy both limits and expands the focus of our war effort. It limits it to the Islamists who have declared jihad against the West. There are many terrorist groups in the world. Many of them are no threat to the United States. If they become a threat, we can so determine it at that time. The current danger is the Islamist one. Naming the threat also expands the scope of our war effort to all the networks of radical Islam, including mosques, schools, and radical Islamic sites on the Internet. It is not only terrorist acts that we are confronting, but also the propaganda and organizations that make them possible.

I understand that President Bush has refused to declare war on the Islamist jihadists in order to avoid inflaming Islamic passions. That decision might have made sense in 2001. But after we have invaded, conquered, and occupied two Muslim nations in two years (policies I strongly supported and continue to support), it is a fair guess that most of the Muslims who are susceptible to being offended by our actions have been offended by now.

I also understand that some people would argue that, following my recommendation, we would be declaring a religious war against more than a billion Muslims. But this is not true—quite the contrary. We would be declaring war on a particular, violent, political ideology within Islam that threatens the West and the health of Muslim societies themselves. By declaring war on the Islamist jihadists now, we can underline why we stand side by side with peaceful and democratic Muslims, and are opposed in Afghanistan and Iraq only by those Muslims who believe in car bombs, terrorism, and murder.

As Jim Hoagland, the *Washington Post's* respected foreign policy columnist, wrote in April 2005: "[It is not] clear that the administration will acknowledge the politically sensitive objective of rolling up the religious networks that produce and support the global jihadists of the Wahhabi, or Salafi, sect of Islam. If not, the Bush team will fight on with one hand tied behind its back."[2]

It is also important to declare war on the Islamist jihadists because we are a nation of laws. When Congress declares war and passes enabling legislation, the president can accept the full authority delegated to him under the Constitution and by Supreme Court precedents that establish presidential powers in wartime. Some such powers that were barely used by President Franklin Roosevelt, like the sedition laws, are necessary to fight our war against Islamist terrorism.

Muslim extremists on the Internet and in mosques openly call for jihad against the United States and Europe. In May 2005, Muslim groups—including the Muslim Council of Britain and the Muslim Parliamentary Association of the UK—gathered in front of the American embassy in London to protest against the United States and Britain. They burned British and American flags and threatened violence, including another September 11 attack, chanting, "USA, watch your back—Osama is coming back" and "Kill, kill USA, kill, kill George Bush" and "Bomb, bomb New York" and "George Bush, you will pay, with your blood, with your head." One protester shouted, "Your so-called democracy will fall under the sword of Allah. The day of judgment is coming!"[3]

If this protest, with its threats of violence and assassination, had been conducted within our own borders, the protesters would have been ripe subjects for sedition prosecutions—and rightly so. Remember, sedition laws do not outlaw dissent, but they do outlaw advocating the violent overthrow of our government and violent opposition to our war effort. The First Amendment has always been construed as permitting such prosecutions during wartime.

It is sometimes argued that unlike less conceptual wars, this War on Terror will go on indefinitely, creating a condition of permanent war, and that any wartime restrictions on civil liberties would be permanent. There is some merit in this concern. But it is equally true that at the beginning of even conventional wars, the end is not known. If Hitler had made a few different decisions (not declared war on the United States, or not invaded Russia, or permitted his armies to retreat from Stalingrad rather than ordering them to stand their ground and be destroyed, or been aware that the Allies had broken his Ultra Code), World War II could have perhaps settled into a stalemate. But when America entered the war, we were committed for as long as it took.

Still, the likely prolonged nature of this war against the Islamist jihadists should be a concern to everyone who values our civil liberties. I would propose that as long as we are inventing a new form of war declaration—not on a foreign government, but on Islamist terrorism—we put a sunset provision on it. Every two years, all exclusively wartime powers would be extinguished and would need to be renewed in a free-standing bill by the next Congress. If a majority of the public was disturbed by a president's use of his war powers, that attitude could be reflected in the next congressional election. Given how difficult it is to pass any significant legislation, requiring congressional approval every two years is a sufficient democratic protection against possible presidential abuse of wartime powers.

Acknowledging reality is a necessary step in winning the war. We are not likely to win this war until we have formally declared it and defined it. Our first step in winning the war is to declare it on the Islamist insurgency.

UTILIZE ETHNIC PROFILING

This brings me to a specific war power that must be available to our government: ethnic/religious profiling. Transportation Secretary Norman Mineta has declared that any profiling taking race, religion, or nationality into account is forbidden in airport security. When CBS's 60 Minutes correspondent Steve Kroft asked him if there were any circumstances in which such profiling would make sense, Secretary Mineta replied, "Absolutely not." When Kroft asked whether an elderly white woman and a young Muslim man should be treated the same, Secretary Mineta responded, "Basically, I would hope so." Kroft then asked, "If you saw three young Arab men sitting, kneeling, praying, before they boarded a flight, getting on, talking to each other in Arabic, getting on the plane, no reason to stop and ask them any questions?" President Bush's secretary of transportation replied, "No reason."4

This is the current policy of the United States government. Our government and its employees cannot take action or make judgments on the basis of ethnicity, religion, or nationality. In fact, our government has severely fined airlines that have barred suspicious-looking Muslim young men from flights.

Obviously, such policies are not based on reason but on political correctness run amok. Various Muslim organizations are quick to hold press conferences and take legal action to intimidate the government regarding the profiling of Muslims. They put pressure on magazines by trying to persuade advertisers to withdraw their ads or face charges of subsidizing racism. They also try to intimidate authors and publishers.

One author who has had the gumption to resist is the courageous Rachel Ehrenfeld, who has written on the role of Saudi money in supporting terrorism. She is currently defending herself in a British court against litigation paid for by a Saudi billionaire.5 Ironically, it is precisely this aggressive defense—by purportedly legitimate and respectable Muslim organizations—of Muslims who are suspected by law enforcement of supporting terrorism that makes the case for ethnic profiling.

During World War II, the internment of German, Italian, and Japanese aliens (and American citizens of Japanese ancestry) was found to be constitutional on the explicit basis that it was reasonable to suspect them of loyalty to a hostile country. Thus, the Supreme Court found that in times of war, the government had the right to protect itself by incarcerating enemy aliens, even though there was no evidence against any individual that he or she was anything other than a loyal resident of the United States.[6] Merely the increased possibility of disloyalty—based on a person's nationality and ethnicity—was sufficient to trigger incarceration or deportation for the duration of the war. (Of course, such an authority was triggered only by a formal declaration of war.)

Today, the question is not incarceration but merely extra attention in sensitive settings, such as boarding an airplane. But special care must be used not only at airports. Our policy must follow the dictates of common sense and national security. For example, since September 11, our government has had a critical shortage of Arabic translators. But according to the testimony of Sibel Dinez Edmonds, a former Arabic translator for the FBI, ambiguous loyalties in the FBI translation office might be compromising our national security.

According to Paul Sperry's book *Infiltration: How Muslim Spies and Subversives Have Penetrated Washington*,[7] when Edmonds reported to work at the FBI a week after September 11, she found ethnic Arab translators in the office celebrating. "It's about time they got a taste of what they've been giving the Middle East," they reportedly said. Her supervisor, an ethnic Arab, instructed her and the rest of the staff of translators to work slowly and let untranslated intercepts pile up. He was promoted to running the Arabic desk, the key position in intercepting the al Qaeda plots, after he threatened to sue the FBI for racial discrimination. Meanwhile, the FBI has instituted bureau-wide Muslim sensitivity training programs for all agents.[8]

Edmonds was fired by the FBI, allegedly because she reported these events. She then sued the government for wrongful dismissal, and her case is currently on appeal. In the trial court, the federal government invoked the State Secrets Privilege to get her case rejected. According to the *Washington Post*, the federal government's demand that the arguments on appeal be closed to the public was "unusual."[9]

The FBI should not be intimidated into politically correct behavior that endangers our security, but this is the natural outcome of policy that puts political correctness before common sense. To give extra scrutiny to Muslims in sensitive situations is not bigotry. If America went to war against England, I would fully expect that as a former Englishman (now a naturalized American citizen), I would receive a thorough background check if I applied for government work or if I wanted to buy a gun or board an airplane. In fact, as a loyal American of English birth and ancestry, I would be outraged if my government didn't take such precautions. In time of war, no loyal American citizen or peaceful resident should resent precautions taken for the common defense. But until we formally declare war against Islamist terrorism and the jihadists who have already declared war on us, the legal basis for such commonsense policies might not be available.

SECURE OUR BORDERS

France's Maginot Line—constructed between 1930 and 1940 to defend against the Germans—was a triumph of shrewd and effective national defense compared to the United States' border policy. The French planned to use their troops to fill the gaps in the Maginot Line, though it turned out that the Germans moved faster than the French, and France lost the war in six weeks. But at least the French had a plan.

The United States has no plan to secure our borders. Our government works hard to keep updated lists of known terrorists, but expects them to enter our country through airports and official border crossing stations. If they, like millions of other illegal aliens, cross our southern or northern border outside of the normal checkpoints, America is utterly exposed.

In 2004, when my colleagues at the *Washington Times* and I interviewed Asa Hutchinson, he was then the senior official at the Department of Homeland Security responsible for securing our borders. He told us it wasn't practical to secure the borders or keep track of illegal immigrants once they entered the country. Shortly after his observation made the front page of our newspaper, Hutchinson was separated from his job. But he was only accurately expressing the government's long-time attitude about the impossibility of controlling America's borders.

A few months later, in December 2004, at a farewell luncheon for Attorney General John Ashcroft, I asked him if, during his four years of service, he had ever seen or heard of any comprehensive study assessing what it would take to substantially secure our borders. He said no.

Yet, on February 16, 2005, Deputy Secretary of Homeland Security James Loy testified in a Senate hearing that, "Recent information from ongoing investigations, detentions, and emerging threat streams strongly suggests that al Qaeda has considered using the southwest border to infiltrate the United States. Several al Qaeda leaders believe operatives can pay their way into the country through Mexico and also believe illegal entry is more advantageous than legal entry for operational security reasons."[10]

Essentially, senior government officials admit both that al Qaeda is planning to illegally sneak terrorists across our borders and that we have no plan for dealing with that likelihood.[11] I don't deprecate the magnitude of the challenge, but in World War II we safely shipped more than ten million troops through submarine-infested seas, built 100,000 combat planes in a single year, and invented and deployed the first atomic bomb. We are at war again and need to treat border security as a necessity. We need to meet the challenge with the same can-do spirit we showed in World War II.

Unfortunately, we seem to have devolved (only temporarily, I trust) from a can-do country to a can't-do country; from a country that does whatever it takes to win to a country that trembles at the possibility that people might think we acted "inappropriately."

Let me tell a little story. When I was a boy, my elementary school held an evening Halloween party for the students and parents. I was standing next to my best friend, and some of the children's mothers had formed in a half-circle around us, chatting happily. Then my friend's costume caught fire from a candle on a nearby table. While we gawked, my friend's dad—who was about thirty yards away from us, talking with my parents—suddenly saw his son on fire. He ran toward him but was blocked by the mothers, who, like me, were frozen in shock. He shoved the women aside, knocking a few of them to the ground, to get to his boy. He quickly put out the fire and saved his son from harm.

For several weeks, the parents spoke scornfully of my friend's dad for slightly bruising the nice women. His dad was (and is) a fine gentleman, a charming and gracious man who knew how to treat a lady. But he was also a former bomber pilot, and when danger struck, he didn't hesitate to kick the nice ladies in the backside to save his boy's life. His generation—the Greatest Generation—instinctively knew that ruthless action trumped pleasant ineffectiveness when danger came knocking at their door. We need to relearn that instinct.

ADOPT NATIONAL IDENTIFICATION CARDS

Here is one hard truth: In the age of terror that we have been drawn into, we can no longer afford the luxury of not requiring national identification cards. Without biometric cards for every person living or traveling in the country, even secured borders will be insufficient. This is a war in which information is king, and the ability to positively identify people is a necessary component of our defense. Fully secured entry into the country requires closely monitored borders backed by universally held biometric cards in the interior.

Millions of people enter our country on tourist visas and then stay and melt into the population. Without biometric cards, millions of such people gain a permanent presence in the United States, and we lose the ability to identify and track them. Often, people who want secure borders are adamant against identification cards. But we can't have effective border security without both.

CHART PROGRESS

I have found nothing as disheartening, since the terrorist attacks of September 11, 2001, as the speed with which complacency has overtaken both the executive and congressional branches of our government.

From my sources in the government, I know there are many individuals—both political appointees and career civil servants—who have not succumbed to the deadly disease of complacency. Particularly in the counter-intelligence and anti-terrorism offices in our government, many patriotic employees work with desperate speed and put in long hours to do their vital jobs. But they work within bureaucracies, and under political or senior civil servant bosses who have fallen back to business as usual, rather than leaning forward to the anti-terrorist business at hand. The same complacency rules under the Capitol dome.

Even on the battlefield, bureaucratic complacency and legal ambiguities have interfered with the execution of the war. In October 2001, Navy captain Shelly Young, a U.S. Central Command lawyer, advised against launching a missile against a vehicle in Afghanistan because women and children might have been in the convoy. That recommendation probably let Mullah Omar, leader of the Taliban and Osama bin Laden's host, escape.[12] This is not a lone case. The legal system has our war effort tangled in knots. The American Civil Liberties Union (ACLU) and other such groups have busily obstructed our war effort by litigating every ambiguity in the law—pursuing their liberal political agendas as usual, regardless of the fact that we are at war.[13] That is their right—until we have formally declared war.

Tellingly, it is not liberal lawyers but anti-terror specialists who are most seized by the urgent nature of the Islamist threat. Worse, the liberal lawyers and supervising bureaucrats exude an air of complacency that is stifling prompt government action. The shining exception to this glum condition was President Bush's and Secretary Rumsfeld's determination to invade Afghanistan within weeks of the September 11 attacks.

The problem of government (and public) complacency is worth a book in itself, but I will give just two examples here.

One issue is the failure to develop and manufacture anti-biological attack vaccines. Project BioShield, as it is called, is a model of unforgivable complacency and delay. Budgeted at $6 billion, it is the largest new Homeland Security program proposed by the White House—strong evidence of the importance the government places on it. Yet here is the timeline for its enactment:

- September 11, 2001: Terrorist attacks on New York and the Pentagon
- September 18, 2001: First reports of biological attack in the form of the anthrax letters delivered to media and government offices
- February 2003: President Bush proposes Project BioShield to develop and manufacture vaccines to protect the public from likely viruses, chemicals, and other pathogens
- July 2004: Congress passes the bill and the president signs it into law

In other words, a year and a half separated the first bioterrorist attack of anthrax, which put us on notice of the danger, and the president's proposal for legislation. Then it took Congress another year and a half to pass the bill. Keep in mind that passage of the legislation does not protect the public at all. It only authorizes and begins to fund the programs that will, in a number of years, dramatically increase our safety.

Three years passed before we even began what the government proposes to fund as its biggest Homeland Security project. By contrast, the World War II Manhattan Project was recommended to FDR by the National Academy of Sciences on, by sheer coincidence, December 6, 1941. By the summer of 1942, FDR had selected Colonel Leslie Groves to run the project. Within three years, Groves had spent the equivalent of $21 billion, hired 130,000 workers, and delivered two usable bombs, which were used to end World War II in the summer of 1945.

That is the difference between complacency and urgency: three years to start a vital project versus three years to complete a vital project.

Complacency also rules in the government's search for reliable translators of Arabic and related languages. In the current war against Islamist terrorism, intelligence is crucial, and words and ideas battle on a daily basis. Yet more than three years after September 11, the FBI admits it has a backlog of 120,000 hours of potentially valuable intercepts. The State Department admits that only one in five of its 279 Arabic translators is fluent enough to manage the subtlety of the language. The military has similar problems.[14]

According to the 9/11 Commission Report: "Despite the recent hire of 653 new linguists, demand exceeds supply. Shortage of translators in languages such as Arabic, Urdu, Farsi, and Pashto remains a barrier to the FBI's understanding of the terrorist threat."[15] The Pentagon admits it is short about two thousand translators.[16]

Aside from classified material left untranslated, there is a much larger domain of what intelligence officials call open sources—newspapers, Internet sites, magazine articles, television and radio broadcasts—that are not even submitted to our translators. And yet the Arabic-language Internet sites are the primary medium for spreading Islamist doctrine and even communicate actual operational information for terrorists.

Further challenging our ability to bring on sufficient translators is the small number of non-Muslim Arabic speakers in America, the risk (or fear) of bias from Muslim translators, and the difficulty of mastering the subtle language to a useful level. All these challenges are formidable, and it is unlikely that we would have sufficient translators even if our government were acting with urgency. But to date, the various agencies that need translators—the CIA, FBI, State Department,

Defense Department, and other agencies—have not changed their methods of acquiring translators. It is still business as usual.

There are hints that federal agencies expect that translating machines will soon replace human translators. But while our government should certainly pursue such technology, we can't rely on it. One of the most damaging habits of our intelligence services has been its overreliance on technology and underreliance on human agents.[17]

What we obviously need are tens of thousands of non-Muslim Arabic translators. There is no evidence that our government is designing a radical new method of recruitment and training to meet this need. Once we needed Russian specialists, now we need Arabic specialists, but our government is not taking the War on Terror as seriously as it took the Cold War.

An urgent mind remains restless until it has solved the problem it faces. A complacent mind takes comfort in how much has been accomplished. And today, almost across the board, our government—and the public—is taking false comfort in marginal but insufficient gains. Our government needs to set aggressive goals, have bureaucrats set real strategies to meet them, and chart—and demand—the progress necessary to achieve these goals with the urgency that wartime requires.

PERFORM FACT-BASED ANALYSIS

"Know thine enemy" is the first guide to warfare, but too much of what we hear about the War on Terror is not about facts but about domestic partisan politics or political ideology. On the populist left there are the conspiracy theories of Michael Moore and the Bush-haters, and at a more intellectual level there are—on the left and right—commentators who see the world through a neo-isolationist prism. The president himself, because he has failed to declare war specifically on the jihadists, has not fully characterized the motivations of Islamist terror.

Within days of September 11, President Bush was asserting that bin Laden's terrorists had attacked us because they hate our love of freedom and our way of life.

The president's so-called "realist" neo-isolationist critics dismissed the president's explanation and declared that bin Laden's motives were a largely rational reaction to our support for Israel and the autocratic petro-regimes of the Middle East. In fact, both Bush and the "realists" are partly right, but their ideological divisions have led the public discussion in the wrong direction, or at least partly wrong.

The entire White House communications apparatus has been largely silent—sometimes for months at a time—and when it talks, it uses clichés that, while true, hardly constitute a full and useful explanation of events. The president's Inaugural and State of the Union Addresses in January 2005 were wonderful exceptions to this rule. But even they addressed only the democracy-building part of the fuller strategy of the war effort.

The failure to effectively communicate with the public is not due to any oratorical shortcomings of the president. Instead, it flows from refusing to name the enemy as the Islamist jihadists. Because of that, the president is unable to outline, explain, and credibly justify his war strategy. And compounding the problem is the White House's ideological refusal to acknowledge that American foreign policy has played a part in inspiring the Islamist jihad against us.

Every American administration since President Truman has recognized and supported Israel's right to exist against Arab assaults, which started at the moment of Israel's birth. During that same period, every

American government has supported Saudi Arabia and the Gulf States, and, in the case of Iran, we overthrew a hostile regime and replaced it with a friendly one in 1954.

Our historic support for Israel remains a moral obligation that is strategically justified. Our support for Muslim petro-regimes remains, at least for a while longer, an economic necessity. But it defies logic to deny that our involvement in the Middle East has not contributed to Islamist opposition to us.

It is important to be honest on this point, because it has deep strategic implications for the war against the Islamist jihadists. President Bush is counting on the democratization of the Middle East to dampen the passions that energize the Islamist war against us. In the long term, his strategy might be the only path to peace. But in the short and middle terms, we might find that popularly elected Muslim governments will oppose us because of our support for Israel, the Saudi oil sheiks, the autocracy of President Mubarak in Egypt, and other governments, and that the number of Islamist terrorists could continue to grow. We might have to deal with the thorns engendered by the policy of democratization before its fruits blossom and mature in a friendlier way.

Significant policy implications flow from this fact. It is possible that, in the near future, every government from Pakistan to Turkey, from Saudi Arabia to Algeria, runs the risk of being governed by Islamists who will use animosity against the United States to inflame its citizens and maintain their loyalty. This isn't an argument to stop supporting our current allies, or semi-allies, in the Muslim world. Our alliance with Pakistan is absolutely necessary. Letting Saudi Arabia, despite its current ambiguous support for terrorism, fall completely into Islamist hands would be a severe setback not only for the United States but for

Europe, Japan, and the rest of the world as well. Turkey has been a historic ally, and it is crucial to try to keep it in the Western world rather than in the Islamist world.

But if things go badly, we need to face the fact that additional American military action might be necessary in the Middle East. Such an honest assessment should determine how large a military we might need, and it is obviously going to have to be larger than the military we have now.

We also need to recognize that the "realists" and neo-isolationists are wrong too. Their argument that we "merely" have to remove our support for Israel and our presence in the Middle East in order to see the motives of the Islamist terrorists dissipate does not reflect the facts, but it does reflect on the neo-isolationists' pre-September 11 opposition to American support of Israel and the Muslim petro-regimes.

The modern theory of Islamist jihad and terrorism was founded in a deep loathing of the American way of life. Osama bin Laden is an intellectual disciple of Sayyid Qutb, the mid-twentieth-century Egyptian intellectual who was executed by the Egyptian government in 1966 and who created the modern Islamist terror doctrine. Qutb came to America in 1948 and left hating all things American. He titled his book *The America I Have Seen*. In it, he claimed he was seduced by a drunken Christian woman and was discriminated against because he was an Arab. He expressed his loathing for American music. He called Christian church services in America "entertainment centers and sexual playgrounds." He condemned America's Indian wars, which he wrote were still ongoing in 1949, and argued that American colonists had driven Hispanic peasants back to Central America before the American Revolution. He called the Revolution "a destructive war led by George Washington."[18]

The entire emotional underpinnings of bin Ladenism are saturated in a loathing of American culture and history. And all this developed *before* America was present in any significant way in the Middle East and before a single dollar or gun had been given to Israel.

The idea that we can somehow peacefully disengage from the Islamist jihad against us by, in essence, appeasing bin Laden's Middle Eastern policy is contradicted by the extreme Islamist hatred of American culture and the fact that Islamist fury is targeted at Europe as well, even though European governments overtly pursue pro-Palestinian, pro-Arab policies. Even if bin Laden is primarily concerned with overturning the Saudi regime and driving the West out of the Middle East, he is only the tip of the sword of the much larger, and growing, Islamist insurgency that seeks to destroy the West.

Bin Laden is a hero of the Islamist insurgency, but individual armed decisions for jihad are being made today by second- and third-generation European Muslims. Their motivation is their contempt and hatred for Western values and lifestyles. Withdrawing our support for Saudi or Israeli governments will not end this hatred. Our continued support of Israel and the Muslim petro-regimes adds fuel to the fire of the Islamist insurgency, but the fire will burn against us regardless. The only honest strategy is not to withdraw, but to defeat the insurgency on the battlefield and in the war of ideas for the mind of the Muslim world.

TAKE ADVANTAGE OF GLOBALIZATION

The globalization—or ever-increasing connectivity—of the world is, to a major degree, both the cause of and the ultimate cure for the Islamist threat. No culture has had a ruder confrontation with the juggernaut of globalization than the Muslim population of the Middle East and Pakistan. Overseen by corrupt and mostly vicious leaders who have enriched themselves in the world oil markets, kept power to themselves, and presided over stagnant economies, the masses of common people—and of Muslims trapped between the two worlds of Western modernity and Islamist ideology—have channeled all their economic, cultural, personal, and political frustrations through the only institution to which they have access: Islam.

Precisely because Islam is the most important institution to these people, Islamic culture has not collapsed in the face of modernity, as other cultures have. Instead, it has gotten stronger and reacted powerfully to the intruding world, and revolutionary leaders like bin Laden have infected this vigorous and angry culture with dangerous pathologies, including Islamist terror and jihad. The insularity and vigor of Islam today poses a severe threat to its host cultures when large numbers of Muslims migrate to Europe, and to a lesser extent the United States and Canada.[19]

It is certainly plausible, and perhaps likely, that as democracy and economic opportunity are introduced into the Middle East, Islamist inflammations might be reduced or eliminated. It is in that sense that globalization (democracy and economic prosperity connected to the larger world) might one day be the cure.

But the dilemma for the West is that, in Islam's current insurgent condition, it is precisely these well-intended connections that outrage some Muslims and threaten the West. So, for example, when we go into Iraq and try to give Iraqis democracy, we simultaneously increase the number of jihadists—at least in the short term—trying to kill Americans who are on a mission of mercy.

The challenge for America and the West is that we must try to, more or less, simultaneously shield our nations from the Islamists; strengthen our own cultural vigor, laws, and military capacity; and shrewdly intervene in the Islamic world to establish healthy economic and political connections. These include creating a free and self-sufficient Iraq and Afghanistan, and perhaps, if the Israelis and Palestinians establish a lasting peace, pouring capital investment into the West Bank to promote mutual prosperity.

The obvious contradiction in these tasks is that to protect ourselves from the Islamists, the pressure will be to strictly limit our connections to Muslim lands and peoples. For example, although Europe has created a continent-wide passport-free zone, the threat of radical Islam could lead to a closer monitoring of borders, restrictions on travel, and reinstituted border checks of both passengers and freight. All this—and looming protectionist sentiment—could substantially reduce the wealth-creating capacity of national economies, perhaps by as much as 10 percent per year. If Europe stops Muslim immigration, which seems likely, and finds grounds to start deporting Muslims (which I suspect will be common within two years), that will act as a further economic depressant in both Europe and the Middle East.

Globalization is both a gift and a curse to mankind. We have increasingly enjoyed the gift these past six decades. If things go badly, we should prepare to endure the curse. But if we use globalization wisely, we might help achieve in the Islamic world what Kemal Atatürk achieved in Turkey—a relatively stable, pro-Western model for Islamic societies.

STRENGTHEN OUR ALLIANCE WITH EUROPE

The best strategy to fend off and reverse the Islamist threat is to strengthen the alliance between the United States and Europe. Of course, Christian Southern Africa (390 million of Africa's approximately

850 million people), Hindu India, non-Muslim Southeast Asia, Christian Latin America, and Russia all have important roles to play in defeating the Islamist jihadists. But a defense of the West without the birthplace of the West—Europe—is almost unthinkable. If Europe becomes Eurabia, it would mean the loss of our cultural and historic first cousins, our closest economic and military allies, and the source of our own civilization. It would be a condition Americans should dread, and should move mountains to avoid.

It bears repeating: An Islamified Europe would be as great a threat to the United States today as a Nazified Europe would have been to the United States in the 1940s. Even before Pearl Harbor, Franklin Roosevelt understood that a Nazi-dominated Europe would be more than a fearsome military and industrial threat; it would be a civilizational threat. Now we face another civilizational threat in insurgent Islam.

Unfortunately, some Americans take Europe's future as an Islamic Eurabia for granted, citing the declining birthrates and church attendance rates of ethnic Europeans. Particularly in conservative circles, there is even a scorn for Europe's future, fueled by resentment of France and Germany's refusal to back us in the Iraq War. France's aggressive effort to block United Nations support for us is a particular source of irritation. At the time, I wrote a few anti-French columns myself—and felt much better for it.

But whatever we might think of Europe's foreign policy machinations, it is a matter of our own national security that we achieve the strongest possible alliance with the strongest possible Europe.

Those who are skeptical of Europe's long-term viability can point to many dangerous European trends. Certainly highest on that list is the large influx of Muslim immigrants into Europe. If that trend continues for the remainder of the twenty-first century, and if the birthrates for

Muslims and Europeans remain constant, the indigenous European population will drop from its current 700 million to barely 200 million, and Muslims will be in the majority.[20]

The second danger that threatens Europe is the dominance of the idea of multiculturalism as a governing principle. Holding every culture as equally valid inevitably undermines national unity and undercuts the love and special respect that Europeans should have for European culture. The well-justified fear is that as hyper-tolerant, or even self-loathing, Europeans are confronted by intolerant, hyper-aggressive Muslims, a Darwinian life-or-death struggle will result in the death of European culture.

In fact, falling European fertility rates are sometimes cited as evidence of a literal European death wish,[21] and the sharp decline in Christian church attendance is seen as, in the words of historian Christopher Dawson, "Europe turning itself into a secular society that has no end beyond its own satisfaction . . . a cancerous growth that will ultimately destroy itself."[22]

And yet, I am quite hopeful that Europe will right itself and become an increasingly more effective and committed ally of the United States in our struggle against the Islamist insurgency. I make this counterintuitive assertion for three reasons. First, we can take it as a general principle that current trends rarely continue indefinitely. Second, because there is growing, if not yet quite compelling, evidence that European attitudes are shifting sharply. And third, because a close examination of the ominous trend line of declining ethnic European birthrates discloses that it doesn't begin to bite until between twenty-five and fifty years from now, when the Islamist ferment might well have abated.

Let me take this last point first. A close examination of the United Nations population data (on which all the dire projections are based) shows that for almost every Western European country and most Eastern European countries, their populations do not even begin to decline until at least 2025. In fact, for the next few decades they continue to go up, even without any new immigration. For example, here are selected country populations for 2005, 2015, 2025, and 2050:

	2005	2015	2025	2050
Austria	8,189,000	8,288,000	8,339,000	8,073,000
Belgium	10,419,000	10,540,000	10,590,000	10,302,000
Germany	82,688,000	82,513,000	81,967,000	78,765,000
Greece	11,120,000	11,233,000	11,173,000	10,742,000
Italy	58,093,000	57,818,000	56,307,000	50,912,000
Romania	21,711,000	20,871,000	19,858,000	16,757,000
Poland	38,530,000	38,110,000	37,095,000	31,916,000

As a point of reference, the numbers for the United States are:

	2005	2015	2025	2050
United States	298,213,000	325,723,000	350,103,000	394,976,000

The numbers for France and Britain also go up slightly in 2025 and 2050, though only because of their larger percentage of Muslim residents.[23]

So for Europe, the trend is slightly up for the next decade, then flat or slightly up or down for 2025, with the numbers only beginning to move decidedly down about fifty years from now. Thus the real problem for Europe during the next half-century is not declining populations but aging populations. And there is some evidence that ethnic European birthrates could rise again. According to polling data, many

Europeans feel intimidated by societal attitudes into having fewer children. A poll published in the German magazine *Eltern*—using a sample of 40,000 respondents—found that 75 percent of Germans wished their society were more friendly to and supportive of parents and children. Hostility in restaurants, the need for better day care and child support services, and other similar concerns were identified as reasons for not having a second or third child. Nevertheless, according to the survey, 89 percent of Germans considered their family the most important part of their lives. Careers came in second at 6 percent. This data at least suggests that it is not suicidal, secular anomie that is driving birthrates lower in Europe, but correctable public attitudes and programs.

Still, with a higher ratio of older to younger people, assuming no new immigration, Europe is likely to run seriously short of workers and taxpayers in the near future. Moving back the retirement age by two to five years would largely solve that problem—at least until 2050.[24]

Of course, the unions and most of Europe's workers strongly oppose any rollback of their early retirement benefits, just as in America polls show that older Americans oppose even the slightest diminution of their Social Security benefits. But over time, cultural values tend to drive policy, and I believe that the most critical decision Europeans are going to make in the twenty-first century is whether they fear Islam more than they fear working a little harder for a little less pay. If the answer is that they fear Islam more, then probably all will come right in Europe. If they fear losing early, fully funded retirement more than they fear growing Muslim populations within their own borders, then we Americans must brace ourselves to stand largely alone to face down the Islamist threat.

To pose the question another way is to ask whether Europeans have become completely, lethally materialistic, or whether the sinews of their history and culture still bind their souls. Do England, Germany, France, Italy, and Belgium mean anything more to their residents than the mere geographic spot they find themselves in? Does patriotism, or even nationalism, still lurk in the European soul? I believe it does, and I believe Europe will recover. The horrors of World War I and World War II, which gave patriotism and nationalism a bad name in Europe, are now fading into the prosaic stories of grandparents and great-grandparents. While those memories fade, the human instinct to rally around your own when threatened by others remains.

Hearteningly, public opinion in Europe is shifting in many regards. As I discussed in earlier chapters, large segments of the public in Holland, Germany, Denmark, Sweden, Britain, and the rest of Europe are turning sharply hostile to further Muslim immigration and to the assertiveness and "un-Europeanness" of much of their existing Muslim population; the issue is not racism or prejudice but a recognition among common Europeans (which is finally filtering up to the most elite European academics and high government bureaucrats and politicians) that multiculturalism is not working.

Fear of multiculturalism might force the entire centralizing project of the European Union to falter. Most observers assume there is an emotional nexus between the rising opposition to the EU's proposed constitution and the proposed admission of Turkey into the EU. Most Europeans do not want a closer relationship with Islam—a religion and culture that increasing numbers of Europeans fear is ever more openly contemptuous of European lifestyles and values. In June 2005, the French and Dutch voters soundly rejected the EU constitution, thus confirming one of the central theses of this book: that 2005 would be a turnaround year for Europe, in which the people would break with the elites and start demanding policies that protect their cultures.

While economic concerns were probably the stronger explicit motive for the people's electoral rebellion in 2005, fear of Islam—in the euphemistic form of the Turkish issue—lurked in the background. But whether it was fear of "Polish plumbers" who would undercut Western European salaries, Muslim immigrants flowing in, or merely a distaste for the supra-national EU determining economic, job, and regulation issues, these votes show the continuing vitality of nationalist and cultural impulses in Europe.

The 55 percent "no" vote of the French and the 63 percent "no" vote of the Dutch mark the first public evidence of the historic discontinuity that I have predicted is about to occur in the West. Whether the European people make the right decisions remains to be seen. But it is now almost certain that they are going to make decisions for themselves.

WIN THE EUROPEAN CULTURE WAR

Will Europe save itself? At the center of that question is whether Europe has turned irredeemably secular and, if it has, whether a secular Europe can rally around any strong, life-affirming values for which it is prepared to fight and die.

No one can know the answer to that question. There has never before existed a major society bereft of religion, and I am inclined to doubt that Europe's center is secular, despite appearances. We have seen that, according to the most reliable EU polling, only 15 percent of Europeans consider themselves agnostics or atheists, and 85 percent claim to hold some spiritual values, (even if fewer than half appear to believe in Christianity). While those numbers are lower than in America and most of the rest of the world, it is a far cry from calling Europe broadly faithless and exclusively secular. It is noteworthy that the Christian faithful are noticeably more prevalent in reliable, anonymous surveys than they are in the church pews. Perhaps they are embarrassed to go. Perhaps the churchmen have done a poor job in their vocation.

Moreover, the extraordinary emotional outpouring in Europe after the death of Pope John Paul II—a pope whose positions on abortion, birth control, homosexuality, and women in the Catholic Church would not seem to hold much appeal for secular Europe—is at least suggestive of some latent connections with the Church among Europeans. Otherwise, what was that all about? Just the death of a famous, friendly old man?

There is certainly anecdotal evidence of the beginning of a revival of faith among European young people. The late Pope John Paul II's many mass rallies and events that reached out to young people seem to have left lasting results. The pope called for a new springtime of evangelization. His efforts might be rewarded.

Michael Naumann, editor of the most influential and widely read weekly in Germany, *Die Zeit*, recently suggested that religion could again play a role in Europe's democratic politics: "The emergence of Evangelical movements in the United States coincides with profound social [and] economic changes. This could happen here too, in so far as if the welfare system were to collapse in Europe, what would people do? In the past we have had totalitarian movements which picked up the unhappiness and discontent. This is not going to happen again, but I think the churches might find it opportune." He adds, "Europeans are of Christian heritage, whether they go to church or not."[25]

In Canada, which is often a cultural halfway house between the U.S. and Europe, the best-known pollster, Reginald Bibby, reported last December that more Canadians, especially young people, are attending church: "Attendance is up by as much as four or five percentage points since the late 1990s.... Lots of people are hurting, struggling to find meaning and worried about their kids.... People are saying, 'Well you know, jeez, I'd like my kids to turn out okay.' If they can find meaning in a church, that makes people feel good about the organization."[26]

A United Press International fact-finding study reported some renewed European interest in the Church:

> There is something afoot in matters of faith, in Germany as in France and other parts of the allegedly de-Christianized continent of Europe, according to Catholic and Protestant clergymen interviewed on a recent fact-finding tour. They spoke of an ever-growing "thirst for God." After leaving Leipzig I received a telephone call from a divinity student. "You won't believe what's going on here," he said. "In this city where only 11 percent belong to a Christian denomination, there are long lines of people outside all churches.... I have never seen this before. Many of these people are very young. They don't know the Lord's Prayer. They don't know the hymns. But they all seemed anxious to come in."[27]

That would seem to indicate both that clergymen have done a miserable job of evangelization and that many Europeans are still open to returning to their religious roots.

Of course Europe is very large, and any number of anecdotes (and there are many similar such reports) is hardly a quantifiable trend. But Michael Naumann's theoretical analysis picks up one of the themes of this book. History advances abruptly. Adversity, in particular, tends to generate dramatic cultural shifts. Naumann's observations reflect the growing awareness in Europe that big, unpleasant changes in its social welfare system are looming. When the inevitable shocks of future terrorist attacks are compounded by the social welfare insecurities that lie ahead, people are likely to do what they have always done in such circumstances: fall back on faith and family.

The surest predictor of a higher birthrate is religion. In Europe, as well as elsewhere, birthrates are highest in families who practice a religion, whether it is Christianity, Islam, or Judaism. Moreover, the welfare state's assurance of retirement care is generally regarded as a factor in reducing birthrates. But if the security of the welfare state collapses, it is likely to trigger a boost in birthrates as a protective hedge against an economically austere old age.

Certainly, the new pope, Benedict XVI, is going to make every effort to rekindle the flame of faith in Europe. He has called on Europe to recover its Christian roots "if it truly wants to survive." He has criticized multiculturalism, "which is so constantly and passionately encouraged and supported, [because it] sometimes amounts to an abandonment and disavowal of what is our own." He has pointed out that "Europe was founded not on geography, but on a common faith. We have to redefine what Europe is, and we cannot stop at positivism." With caution, Pope Benedict has also stood up to Islam, speaking in defense of the rights of converts from Islam to Christianity, and he has approved Christian proselytizing of Muslims. In addition, he has opposed Turkey's entry into the EU because it is not a Christian country.[28]

American Protestant missionaries should join the pope in re-evangelizing Europe. After all, over the last thirty years American evangelists have brought millions of highly educated Americans to the faith. Many of these Americans were just as secular as Europeans are today. If in the last century, so full of Marxism, Freudianism, and atheism, Christianity could convert such clever minds as G. K.

Chesterton, T. S. Eliot, C. S. Lewis, Evelyn Waugh, Graham Greene, and Malcolm Muggeridge, there is no reason to fear that converts cannot be made in Europe today. We won't know Europe's religious potential until an effort has been made to evangelize it—and no such major effort has been made since the 1950s.

But even if Europeans remain fully secular and indifferent to their religious heritage, they can still be effective allies against Islamist terror. To some extent, it is a conceit of churchgoers that people cannot find transcendent values worth living or dying for outside of religion. The twentieth century is scarlet red with the blood willingly sacrificed by irreligious socialists, National Socialists, Communists, and anarchists. And, of course, countless European and American soldiers, religious and otherwise, fought against the tyrannies of the Nazis and the Imperial Japanese.

When a French prime minister opposes Turkey's entrance into the EU on the grounds that it would taint the "secular" nature of Europe, we can see that there are more grounds on which to oppose the Islamists than simply a religious "clash of civilizations." While religion is probably the most powerful force in determining a culture's strength, it is not the only one. Love of country, loyalty to a homeland and a way of life, even hatred of other ways, are also powerful cultural forces around which to rally. Throughout history, people have sacrificed and fought for their country—including if that country was atheistic, revolutionary France or atheistic, Stalinist Russia.

But to a measurable extent, the most secular and most anti-Christian elements in Europe are largely the boomer radicals of the 1960s generation. Prudence, at the least, would suggest that we forbear from making a final judgment on an entire continental civilization based on the attitude of one particularly aggressive and disruptive generation. George

Weigel, the Catholic scholar and official biographer of Pope John Paul II, points out in his shrewd and elegant book *The Cube and the Cathedral: Europe, America, and Politics Without God*, that it is the 1960s radicals who are the "driving force behind the radical secularism that has become the ruling ideology of the European Union. By turning their back on Europe's Christian patrimony... the disillusioned radicals of the 1960s are struggling to make sense of a world where, especially since the revolution of 1989 [the fall of Communism], they seem to have lost the plot. The church is their scapegoat for Auschwitz, for the failure of the left, and for the fact that their children are, in many cases, rejecting their values and even turning to religion."[29]

THE COMMON DEFENSE

Whichever way Europe turns, American foreign policy should engage it much more comprehensively and profoundly. We need to guide Europeans to become the most effective allies they can be in this war. There will be times, of course, such as in the Iraq War, when we must act without united European support. But it has been a mistake of strategic dimensions to have exacerbated, rather than ameliorated, the unavoidable divisions we had with Europe over Iraq.

It is startling how quickly, and on how little evidence, Europeans and Americans have declared their separate cultural ways. I would argue that there is at least as big a cultural divide between Manhattan and Memphis as there is between Western Europe and America. The binding common traditions of language, religion, history, politics, foods, styles of life, and love of individual freedom are sufficient to form a lasting alliance between Americans and Europeans, from Boise to Budapest, from Chicago to Seville. The historic force of the Islamist insurgency, if nothing else, should hammer us back into a common sword that we can call the West.

We are living through a historic moment, and despite the uncertainty of these world-changing events, we have good reason to believe that we will emerge a stronger, more united people, optimistic about our future. We still have it within our power to navigate through the storm engendered by insurgent Islam.

The United States is the wealthiest, most powerful nation on earth, a condition we have attained by our historic capacity to enthusiastically solve problems and take advantage of changing circumstances. It's a set of habits that earned us the catchphrase "the can-do American spirit." Although we are Providentially situated (and, we hope, guided), it has nonetheless been our abilities as a practical people that have brought us so far. The only truly original American school of philosophy has been Pragmatism, a philosophy that judges truth by its practical effects. Unburdened by ancient animosities, ideologies, and fears, we have been and remain a broadly religious people with an abiding faith in practically applied reason.

The challenge before us is simply to see the world as we usually have—with our eyes wide open and applying our good, practical common sense to the managing of it.

Over the last fifty years, our immense power and wealth have cushioned us and our European allies from the necessity of taking an accurate measure of the world around us. In the past, we have had the luxury of possessing a wide margin for error. Many mistakes and misjudgments have been barely noticed. We even mismanaged and lost the Vietnam War without any appreciable negative effect on our place in the world (except, of course, for those young soldiers of ours who sacrificed so much for so little gratitude).

What is different now is that we have lost most of our margin for error. We have to get our plan right and execute it very well. Big mistakes no longer have small costs. Even in the Cold War, traditional nation-state restraints on governments kept the world from going to the brink of nuclear war more than once. But in the Age of Terror, our enemies know no restraint, and small mistakes can have catastrophic costs. We can no longer indulge happy fantasies of perpetual safety. We can no longer sacrifice good judgment and needed policy to the conceit of political correctness. We must act today as if the dangers the experts expect to happen will actually happen soon.

If we act properly, if the United States and Europe act together as the West, in defense of our common values, we can undo the nightmare scenario of the Islamists and defeat this new threat of global tyranny that is as every bit as real and dangerous as the Nazi threat that the Greatest Generation met and extinguished more than fifty years ago.

The West stood together then against the forces of barbarism. We need to do so again.

POSTSCRIPT

In late December 1941, the United States government made the decision to order over thirty thousand troops in the Philippines to fight a holding action to buy time for America's broader war operations. By that action in Bataan, we kept Manila Bay from the Japanese enemy for five months.

Those five months were purchased at the price of thirty thousand American soldiers killed or imprisoned. As General MacArthur said at the time, "We must die in our tracks, falling not backward but forward toward the enemy."[30] In war, time can be that valuable.

Today, in the first four years of our war against Islamist terrorism, when time could have been purchased at a far cheaper price, we have squandered it. What price in American lives will we eventually pay for the time we are wasting today?

Acknowledgments

I wish to express my appreciation to my editor, Harry Crocker, for his good counsel and encouragement. I appreciate the help of all the folks at Regnery. I particularly want to thank my friend John Roberts, an investigative reporter and art historian, for his invaluable assistance on the subject of European and Islamic art.

I am so deeply appreciative of my wife, Lynda, and our children, Spencer, Trevor, and Anastasia, for their constant love and support.

Finally I want to express my gratitude to the four of our ten cats—Tourquoise, Crooker, Bosnica, and Junior—who kept me company in my library while I was writing this book (even if they sometimes stepped on the delete key—perhaps not often enough).

Bibliography

Alexander, Col. John B. *Winning the War*. New York: Thomas Dunne Books, 2003.

Baker, Raymond William. *Islam without Fear*. Cambridge: Harvard University Press, 2003.

Baran, Zeyno. *Hizb Ut-Tahrir: Islam's Political Insurgency*. Washington, D.C.: The Nixon Center, 2004.

Barnett, Roger W. *Asymmetrical Warfare*. Washington, D.C.: Brassey's Inc, 2003.

Barnett, Thomas P. M. *The Pentagon's New Map*. New York: G.P. Putnam's Sons, 2004.

Booker, Christopher, and Richard North. *The Great Deception*. New York: Continuum, 2003.

Burns, James MacGregor. *The Crosswinds of Freedom*. New York: Alfred A. Knopf, 1989.

Delsol, Chantal. *Icarus Fallen*. Wilmington: ISI Books, 2003.

Diamond, Jared. *Collapse*. New York: Viking, 2005.

Ehrenfeld, Rachel. *Funding Evil*. Santa Monica: Bonus Books, 2005.

Evans, Richard J. *The Coming of the Third Reich*. New York: Penguin Press, 2004.

Fleming, Thomas. *The New Dealers' War*. New York: Basic Books, 2001.

Friedman, Yohanan. *Tolerance and Coercion in Islam*. Cambridge: Cambridge University Press, 2003.

Fromkin, David. *Europe's Last Summer*. New York: Alfred A. Knopf, 2004.

Fuller, Graham E. *The Future of Political Islam*. New York: Palgrave Macmillan, 2003.

Gaddis, John Lewis. *Surprise, Security, and the American Experience*. Cambridge: Harvard University Press, 2004.

Gray, John. *False Dawn*. New York: The New Press, 1998.

Guillemin, Jeanne. *Biological Weapons*. New York: Columbia University Press, 2005.

Harari, Haim. *A View from the Eye of the Storm*. New York: Regan Books, 2005.

Harris, Lee. *Civilization and Its Enemies*. New York: Free Press, 2004.

Herf, Jeffrey. *Reactionary Modernism*. New York: Cambridge University Press, 1984.

Higgs, Robert. *Crisis and Leviathan*. New York: Oxford University Press, 1987.

Himmelfarb, Gertrude. *The De-Moralization of Society*. New York: Alfred A. Knopf, 1995.

———. *The Roads to Modernity*. New York: Alfred A. Knopf, 2004.

Hourani, Albert. *A History of the Arab Peoples*. Cambridge: The Belknap Press of Harvard University Press, 1991.

Huggins, Laura E., and Hanna Skandera. *Population Puzzle*. Stanford: Hoover Institution Press, 2004.

Jackall, Robert. *Propaganda*. New York: New York University Press, 1995.

Kater, Michael H. *Hitler Youth*. Cambridge: Harvard University Press, 2004.

Keefe, Patrick Radden. *Chatter*. New York: Random House, 2005.

Kepel, Gilles. *The War for the Muslim Minds*. Cambridge: The Belknap Press of Harvard University Press, 2004.

Kotlikoff, Laurence J., and Scott Burns. *The Coming Generational Storm*. Cambridge: M.I.T. Press, 2004.

Kushner, Harvey. *Holy War on the Home Front*. New York: Sentinel, 2004.

Larrabee, Eric. *Commander in Chief*. New York: Harper and Row, 1987.

Levy, Barry S., and Victor W. Sidel. *Terrorism and Public Health*. New York: Oxford University Press, 2003.

Lewis, Bernard. *The Middle East*. New York: Touchstone, 1995.

———. *What Went Wrong*. New York: Perennial, 2002.

Linfield, Michael. *Freedom under Fire*. Boston: South End Press, 1990.

Malkin, Michelle. *In Defense of Internment*. Washington, D.C.: Regnery, 2004.

McGrath, Alister. *The Future of Christianity*. Malden: Blackwell Publishers, 2002.

———. *The Twilight of Atheism*. New York: Doubleday, 2004.

Nisbet, Robert. *History of the Idea of Progress*. New York: Basic Books, 1980.

Orwell, George. *An Age Like This*. New York: Harcourt Brace Jovanovich, 1968.

Rehnquist, William H. *All the Laws But One*. New York: Vintage, 1998.

Roberson, B. A. *Shaping the Current Islamic Reformation*. Portland: Frank Cass Publishers, 2003.

Roy, Olivier. *Globalized Islam*. New York: Columbia University Press, 2004.

Safi, Omid. *Progressive Muslims*. Oxford: One World, 2003.

Scheuer, Michael. *Imperial Hubris*. Washington, D.C.: Brassey's, Inc., 2004.

Schlesinger Jr., Arthur M. *The Disuniting of America*. New York: W.W. Norton & Company, 1992.

Schneier, Bruce. *Beyond Fear*. New York: Copernicus Books, 2003.

Schram, Martin. *Avoiding Armageddon*. New York: Basic Books, 2003.

Spencer, Robert. *Onward Muslim Soldiers*. Washington D.C.: Regnery, 2003.

Sperry, Paul. *Infiltration*. Nashville: Nelson Current, 2005.

Van Creveld, Martin. *The Transformation of War*. New York: The Free Press, 1991.

Weil, Simone. *The Need for Roots*. London: Routledge Classics, 2002.

Wiebe, Robert H. *Who We Are*. Princeton: Princeton University Press, 2002.

Wiggershaus, Rolf. *The Frankfurt School*. Cambridge: The M.I.T. Press, 1995.

Ye'or, Bat. *Eurabia*. Cransbury: Associated University Presses, 2005.

Notes

Chapter Two: Hope and Determination

1   According to the Catholic Encyclopedia, "The conception of Europe as a distinct division of the earth, separate from Asia and Africa, had its origin in ancient times. The sailors of the Aegean Sea applied the Semitic designations Ereb (sunset, west) and Acu (sunrise, east) to the countries lying respectively west and east of the sea; in this way it became customary to call Greece and the territory back of it Europe, while Asia Minor and the parts beyond were named Asia. At a later date the mass of land lying to the south of the Mediterranean was set off as a distinct division of the earth with the name of Libya or Africa." See "Europe" in *The Catholic Encyclopedia* (Encyclopedia Press, published in 16 volumes, 1912).

2   Noam Chomsky, "Bilinguistics and the Human Capacity" (lecture, MTA, Budapest, May, 17, 2004) quoting Nobel Laureate

Salvador Luria from a 1974 symposium, http://www.nyrud.hu/ chomsky/lect.html.

3 Or consider the phrase "home ownership" presented to a primitive, nomadic tribe that had no concept of personal property. The phrase would introduce something that they had never imagined before.

4 William H. Rehnquist, *All the Laws But One* (New York: Vintage Books, 1998), 219.

5 William S. Lind and others, "The Changing Face of War: Into the Fourth Generation," *Marine Corps Gazette*, October 1989, 22–26.

6 Abraham Lincoln's message to Congress, December 1, 1862.

Chapter Three: The Threat

1 Olivier Roy, *Globalized Islam* (New York: Columbia University Press, 2004), 41.

2 "Radical Islamism in Europe": Interview with Irshad Manji, Steven Emerson, and Gilles Kepel. http://www.aspenberlin.org/ special_feature.php?iGedminid=8.

3 Michael Kater, *Hitler Youth* (Cambridge, MA: Harvard University Press, 2004), 29.

4 Richard Evans, *The Coming of the Third Reich* (New York: Penguin, 2004).

5 The earliest public use of the phrase I could find was by radio host Michael Savage and journalist Christopher Hitchens, but it is now increasingly used by conservatives

6 Roy, 294–313.

7 Gilles Kepel, *The War for Muslim Minds* (Cambridge, MA: Belknap, 2004), 288–89.

8   Thomas Friedman, "Divided We Stand," *New York Times*, January 23, 2005.

9   Kepel, 256.

10   Roy, 317.

11   Kepel, 243.

12   "Police Urged to Reopen 'Honour Killing' Cases," *London Daily Telegraph*, June 12, 2004.

13   Sean O'Neil and Kaakov Lappin, "Britain's Online Imam Declares War as He Calls Young to Jihad," *London Times*, January 17, 2005.

14   Ibid.

15   Nicola Woolcock, "Muslim Group Targets Poster," *London Times*, January 22, 2005.

16   "German Intelligence Says Islamists Present Major Threat," *Deutsche Welle*, May 18, 2004.

17   "A Growing Muslim Minority Is Challenging Europe's View of Itself," *U.S. News & World Report*, January 10, 2005.

18   "Most Imams Boycotted Muslim Anti-violence Protest March," *Norway Post*, December 5, 2004.

19   Farzana Hassan-Shahid, "Are Opponents of Shariah Anti-Islam?" *Muslim Wake Up!* February 8, 2005.

20   Kepel, 241; B. A. Roberson, *Shaping the Current Islamic Reformation* (London: Frank Cass Publishers, 2003), 82–142.

21   This book is focused on how the West is thinking about and dealing with the Islamist threat—it is not intended as a detailed description or analysis of the mechanics of terrorism. There are many excellent recent books on that subject. Readers should see Harvey Kushner's *Holy War on the Home Front: The Secret Islamic Terror Network in the United States* and Robert Spencer's *Onward*

Muslim Soldiers: How Jihad Still Threatens America and the West. For a superb analysis of the threat of biological, chemical, and nuclear terrorism, readers should see Martin Schram's *Avoiding Armageddon*, written in conjunction with PBS's eight-part series of the same title.

22   *Imperial Hubris* (Washington, DC: Brassey's, 2004), 160–61.

23   Ibid., 241.

24   "Interpol Sounds Bioterror Alarm," BBC, February 23, 2005.

25   Ibid.

26   John Steele, "Terror Threat from 'Very Many' Muslim Men, Says Met Chief," *London Telegraph*, March 3, 2005.

27   See generally Harvey Kushner's *Holy War on the Home Front: The Secret Islamic Terror Network in the United States* and Robert Spencer's *Onward Muslim Soldiers: How Jihad Still Threatens America and the West.*

28   Jerry Seper, "Border to Remain Unprotected," *Washington Times*, September 10, 2004.

29   Council on Foreign Relations document, "Terrorism: Questions and Answers," January 7, 2004. http://cfrterrorism.org/weapons/dirtybomb.html.

30   Barry S. Levy and Victor W. Sidel, eds., *Terrorism and Public Health* (New York: Oxford University Press in cooperation with American Public Health Association, 2003), 220–45. See also the 2004 BBC production "Dirty Bomb."

31   Schram, 202.

32   Ibid., 201.

33   "High risk of WMD attack in decade," CNN, June 25, 2005.

Chapter Four: Europe Reacts

1   Ronald Rovers, "The Silencing of Theo van Gogh," Salon.com, November 24, 2004, http://archive.salon.com/news/feature/2004/11/24/vangogh/.

2   Mona Charen, "The Knife's Message," Townhall.com, November 19, 2004, http://www.townhall.com/columnists/monacharen/mc20041119.shtml.

3   Charles Bremner, "Stoned to Death: Why Europe Is Starting to Lose Faith in Islam," *London Times*, December 4, 2004.

4   Carol Eisenberg, "Immigration Becomes Political," *Newsday*, December 6, 2004.

5   Christopher Caldwell, "The Dutch Rethink Multiculturalism," *Weekly Standard*, December 27, 2004.

6   "Europe Gets Tough with Islamists," Penraker.com, December 4, 2004, http://www.penraker.com/archives/000911.html.

7   Bremner, "Stoned to Death."

8   "FOX News on Malmö, Sweden," Dhimmi Watch, October 28, 2004, http://www.jihadwatch.org/dhimmiwatch/archives/003692.php.

9   "France Pulls Plug on Ardo Network," BBC News, December 14, 2004.

10   "Integration Debate Heats up in Germany," *Deutsche Welle*, November 20, 2004.

11   He got more votes than the winner Gerhard Schröder in the last general election, but the Green Party supported Schröder in a coalition government.

12   Hannah Cleaver, "Turkish Workers a Mistake, Claims Schmidt," *London Telegraph*, November 25, 2004.

13   George Jones, "Howard: Why Britain Must Get Quotes on Immigration," *London Telegraph*, January 24, 2005.

14   Charles Moore, "The Spectator's Notes," *Spectator*, April 30, 2005, 11.

15   The polling sample of 1989 respondents is almost twice as large as a valid national sample for the United States, with five times the population—so there is clearly nothing wrong with the sample size.

Chapter Five: The Deracination of the West

1   George MacDonald Fraser, *The Light's on at Signpost* (Guilford, CT: Lyons Press, 2004).

2   Robert Nisbet, *History of the Idea of Progress* (New York: Basic Books, 1980), 5.

3   See Rolf Wiggershaus, *The Frankfurt School, Its History, Theories and Political Significance* (Cambridge, MA: MIT Press, 1995).

4   James W. Caeser and Patrick J. McGuinn, *Public Interest*, fall 1998.

5   James Burnham, *The Suicide of the West: An Essay on the Meaning and Destiny of Liberalism* (Washington, DC: Regnery, 1985), 24–26.

6   Ibid.

Chapter Six: Saving Democracy, 1940s Style

1   Thomas Fleming, *The New Dealers' War: FDR and the War within World War II* (New York: Basic Books, 2002), 112.

2   Ibid., 193.

3   Mark Landy and Sidney Milkis, *Presidential Greatness* (Lawrence, KS: University Press of Kansas, 2000), 191.

4   *New Yorker*, June 1, 1940.

5   William H. Rehnquist, *All the Laws But One* (New York: Vintage Books, 2000), 221–22.

6   For purists, Britain was and is a constitutional monarchy and the United States was and is a constitutional republic.

7   Eric Larrabee, *Commander in Chief: Franklin Delano Roosevelt, His Lieutenants and Their War* (New York: Harper & Row, 1987), 10.

8   I don't mean to ignore the massive and heroic contribution of the Russian people to the successful war effort. But as they were ruled by a Communist government, their domestic policies can be no guide to us today as we try to judge how our democracy should fight our great struggle.

9   The OSS was the precursor to the CIA.

10 Robert Jackall, ed., *Propaganda* (New York: New York University Press, 1995), 229–34.

11 Paul Fussell, *Wartime* (New York: Oxford University Press, 1989).

12 Gottschalk, "Consistent with Security: History of American Military Press Censorship," *Communications & Law*, 39; Michael Linfield, *Freedom Under Fire* (Boston: South End Books, 1990).

13 "Censor's Office Works Smoothly on War News," *Editor and Publisher*, 75:9 (February 21, 1942).

14 Linfield, 72.

15 7 Fed. Reg. 1499–1501 (February 20, 1942), and see generally Linfield.

16 Linfield, 71.

17 Linfield, 73; Summers, 164.

18 Allan M. Winkler, *The Politics of Propaganda: The Office of War Information, 1942–1945* (New Haven: Yale University Press, 1978); Theodore Koop, *Weapon of Silence* (Chicago: University of

Chicago Press, 1946); Charles J. Tull, *Father Coughlin and the New Deal* (Syracuse: Syria University Press, 1965).

19 Richard Polenberg, *War and Society: The United States, 1941–1945* (Philadelphia: J.P. Lippincott, 1972), and John Morton Blum, *V Was For Victory: Politics and American Culture During World War II* (New York: Harcourt Brace Jovanovich, 1976); Richard W. Steele, "Franklin D. Roosevelt and His Foreign Policy Critics," *Political Science Quarterly*, 94 (Spring 1979), 15-3; *The Annual Reports of the American Civil Liberties Union*, Vol. 3, July 1937–June 1944, and Vol. 4, July 1944–December 1950 (New York: Arno Press, 1970); One should also examine *In Brief Authority* (Garden City, NY: Doubleday, 1962), the memoirs of Francis Biddle, FDR's wartime attorney general.

20 Final report of the Senate Select Committee to Study Governmental Operations with Respect to Intelligence Activities, April 23, 1976.

21 Ibid.

22 Ibid., note 181.

23 Ibid., note 170.

24 See Michelle Malkin, *In Defense of Internment* (Washington, DC: Regnery, 2004), 53–54.

25 Johnson v. Eisentrager, 339 U.S. 763 (1950).

26 See Chapter Eight, "Al Qaeda Gets a Lawyer," in Mark R. Levin, *Men in Black* (Washington, DC: Regnery, 2005).

27 Hughes, "War Powers Under the Constitution," 42 ABA Rep 232;238.

28 Ibid., 320 US 81, 95.

29 Ibid., 99.

30 Rehnquist, 207.

31   40 Stat, 555 (1918; 40 Stat. 217 (1917)).

32   Nathan Williams, "How has the onset of war coincided with lim-
      itations on press freedom throughout our nation's history?" His-
      tory NewsNetwork, October 12, 2001.

33   Linfield, 29.

34   *Ft. Minersville School Dist.* v. *Gobitis* (310 U.S. 586).

35   Ibid., 595.

36   Ibid., 596.

37   Ibid.

38   Linfield, 77.

39   Majority opinion of Chief Justice Vinson.

Chapter Seven: A World in Transition

1   George Orwell, *My Country Right or Left, 1940–1943* (New York:
      Harcourt Brace Jovanovich, 1968), 15.

2   David Fromkin, *Europe's Last Summer* (New York: Knopf, 2004),
      143.

3   Ibid., 187–88.

4   Buchanan, James, *Encyclopedia Britannica*, http://www.britanica.com
      /eb/article?tocld 1 9017867.

5   Testimony of Trustee Thomas Saving, February 17, 2005, before
      the Senate Budget Committee.

6   Conversation on background at the Caucus Room restaurant,
      Washington, D.C., April 14, 2005.

7   *Washington Times,* April 10, 2005.

8   Laura E. Huggins and Hanna Skandera, *Population Puzzle: Boom
      or Bust?* (Stanford, CA: Hoover Institution Press, 2005).

9   Reprint, Cutchogue, NY: Buccaneer Books, 1997.

10   Huggins and Skandera, 23.

11   Ibid., 354.

12   Nicholas Eberstadt, "World Population Trends," *The Australian Family* (July 2000), 24.

13   Ibid., 11.

14   Ibid., 10–15.

15   *Deutsche Welle*, January 2, 2005, www.dw-world.de/dw/article/0,1564,1456796.00html.

16   *Deutsche Welle*, January 1, 2005, www.dw0world.de/dw/article/0,1564,1442681,00.html.

17   Ibid.

18   Jon Henley, "French poll shows depth of hostility to Turkey," *Guardian Unlimited*, September 29, 2004.

19   "Anti-Muslim bias spreads in EU," *Turkish Weekly*, March 3, 2005.

20   "Immigrants worry leading nations," Associated Press, May 26, 2004.

21   He was crown prince of the Habsburg monarchy from 1916–1918. His uncle Archduke Franz Ferdinand was assassinated in Sarajevo in 1914, precipitating World War I. His father, Charles, was the last Habsburg emperor (1916–1918) and was beatified by Pope John Paul II on October 3, 2004.

22   Interview with Otto von Habsburg, Washington Times, April 11, 2005.

23   http://evs.kub.nl.

24   European Values Study: Selected Results, Russian Public Opinion & Market Research; http://www.romir.ru/eng/research/01_2001/europe-values.htm.

25   Ibid.

26   BBC European news, April 22, 2002.

27   Ibid.

28 "Is Europe one big blue state?" *Christian Science Monitor*, February 22, 2005.

29 Gallup International Millennium Survey.

30 Ibid.

31 As reported at Christianity.ca, Canada's Christian Community online, at http://christinity.ca/news/commentary/2005/01.005. html.

32 Worldwide Adherents of All Religions by Six Continental Areas, Mid-2003, in "Religion," *Encyclopedia Britannica*, 2004 *Encyclopedia Britannica* Online, November 20, 2004, http://search.eb.com/ eb/article?tocld=9396555.

33 George Weigel, "Christian evangelization: Asia dawn?" *The Tidings*, http://www.the-tidings.com/2004/0109/difference.htm.

34 http://www.cbn.com/CBNNews/News/030819a.asp. See also David Aikman, *Jesus in Beijing: How Christianity Is Transforming China and Changing the Global Balance of Power* (Washington, DC: Regnery, 2003).

35 Karl Marx, *Introduction to a Contribution to the Critique of Hegel's Philosophy of Right*, 1844.

36 http://www.artsci.wustl.edu/anthro/blurb/b_boyer.html.

37 "Tests of Faith," *Guardian*, February 24, 2005.

Chapter Eight: The Way Forward

1 Martin Schram, *Avoiding Armageddon* (New York: Basic Books, 2003), 204–09).

2 Jim Hoagland, "A Shifting Focus on Terrorism," *Washington Post*, April 24, 2005.

3 http://www.thisislondon.com/news/articles/18759971?source= PA&ct=5.

4   Michelle Malkin, *In Defense of Internment* (Washington, DC: Regnery, 2004), xxii.

5   Rachel Ehrenfeld, *Funding Evil* (New York: Bonus Books, 2004), xi–xiv.

6   William Rehnquist, *All the Laws But One* (New York: Vintage, 1998), 184–205; see also Malkin.

7   Paul Sperry, *Infiltration: How Muslim Spies and Subversives Have Penetrated Washington* (Nashville, TN: Nelson Current, 2005).

8   Ibid., xv–xvi.

9   "Hearing in FBI Translator's Case Remains Closed," *Washington Post*, April 22, 2005.

10   Shaun Waterman, "Analysis: Porous borders a back door for terrorists?" *Washington Times*, March 14, 2005.

11   In the late spring of 2005, according to a confidential senior source in the Department of Homeland Security, a comprehensive plan for securing both the two-thousand-mile Mexican border and the four-thousand-mile Canadian border had been developed. But as this book goes to press, it has not yet been raised to the senior departmental and White House level for endorsement and action.

12   Col. John Alexander, *Winning the War* (New York: Thomas Dunne Books, 2003), 253.

13   See Chapter Eight, "Al Qaeda Gets a Lawyer," in Mark Levin, *Men in Black* (Washington, DC: Regnery, 2005).

14   "The Price of Homophobia," *New York Times*, January 20, 2005.

15   Counter Intelligence and Intelligence collection, staff statement #12, "Reforming Law Enforcement," *The 9/11 Commission Report* (New York: W. W. Norton, 2004).

16 Testimony of Lelita Long, deputy undersecretary of defense for policy, at the House Intelligence Committee hearing, February 26, 2004.

17 Patrick Radden Keefe, *Chatter* (New York: Random House, 2005), 128–32.

18 Sayyid Qutb, *America*, http://www.npr.org/templates/story/story.php?storyId=1253796; "Is this the man who inspired bin Laden?" *Guardian Unlimited*, November 1, 2001.

19 The East Asian component of Islam—including the Islamist insurgency in the Philippines—is beyond the scope of this book.

20 Pat Buchanan, *Death of the West* (New York: St. Martin's Press, 2002), 14–24.

21 Actually, the average European woman has about 1.4 babies; 2.01 is the replacement rate. So most people are deciding to have babies, just closer to one rather than two, on average. The average European family is not childless, just small. In attempting to understand the psychology of declining birth rates, it is important to factor in the reality that most Europeans still decide to have at least one child. So it is not literally a death wish or a desire not to reproduce.

22 Daniel Johnson, "Europe's Apocalypse," *New York Sun*, April 11, 2005.

23 World Population Prospects: The 2004 Revisions, http://www.geohive.com/global/pop_data4.php.

24 I would point out that when Bismarck established Germany's social security system in 1875, the retirement age was seventy. And that was in an industrial age of hard labor, not a post-industrial age of service jobs that are easier on the body.

25   http://www.radio.cz/en/article/60271, December 11, 2004.

26   Eric Schakleton, "Canadians, especially young people, are return-
     ing to church, says sociologist," *Canadian Press*, December 28,
     2004.

27   http://powerlineblog.com/archives/005503.php, December 28,
     2003.

28   Robert Spencer, "Pope Benedict XVI: Enemy of Jihad,"
     http://www.FrontPageMagazine.com, April 20, 2005.

29   Johnson, "Europe's Apocalypse."

30   Louis Morton, *The Fall of the Philippines: The U.S. Army in WWII*
     (Washington, DC: 1953), 160, 171.

Index

A

abortion, 37, 191

Achaemenid Dynasty, 22

Adorno, Theodor, 100

Adrianople, 23

Afghanistan, 8, 29, 64; bin Laden, Osama in, 24; War on Terror and, 30, 31, 137

Africa, 147, 184–85; Christianity in, 157; Islamic violence in, 38

Against All Enemies (Clarke), 59–60

Age of Discovery, 23, 135–36

Agence France-Presse, 84

AIDS, 81

al Jazeera, 9, 49, 88, 109

al Manor, 81

al Qaeda: bioterrorism and, 63, 66; border security and, 172–73; European Muslims and, 52; nuclear weapons and, 64; terror-ism and, 44; in United States, 63; War on Terror and, 36–37

Algeria, 69, 147, 180

Ali, Ayaan Hirsi, 73–74

"All Things Considered" (NPR), 74–75

Allievi, Stefano, 88

The America I Have Seen (Qutb), 180

American Civil Liberties Union (ACLU), 175

American Indians, 32–33, 131

American Muslims: assimilation of, 25; Election 2008 and, 10–17; sharia and, 13–18. *See also* European Muslims; Muslims

American Revolution, 180

anthrax, 66, 176

anti-Americanism, 44

Anti-terrorism Crime and Security Act, 52

appeasement, 107
Aquinas, Saint Thomas, 135
Arafat, Yasser, 77
art, offensive displays of, 1–8
Ashcroft, John, 172
Asia, 185; Christianity in, 157; Islamic violence in, 38
Aspen Institute, 45
Asquith, Herbert, 133, 134
Atatürk, Mustafa Kemal, 151–52, 184
Austria, 23, 187
Axis of Evil, 30

B

Bacon, Roger, 135
Baldwin, Stanley, 144
Balkan Peninsula, 23, 57
Bangladesh, 147
Baptists, 15
Baran, Zeyno, 44
Battle of Issus (333 B.C.), 22
Bavarian Christian Social Union, 76
Beaubourg, France, 5
Belgium, 7, 187
Bellow, Saul, 100
Beltway snipers (2002), 63
Benedict XVI, 192
Benjamin, Walter, 100
Berlin and Brandenburg Turkish Association, 83
Berliner Zeitung, 74
Beslan, Russia, 73, 85, 105
Bibby, Reginald, 191–92
Bible, 45
Biddle, Francis, 107
bin Laden, Osama, 23, 61, 92, 109, 167; in Afghanistan, 24; Bush,

George W. and, 179; compliance with, 60, 61; economic war and, 139; jihad and, 42, 49, 180; Middle Eastern policy of, 182; terrorism and, 63–64; as threat to United States, 35; War on Terror and, 36–37
bioterrorism: al Qaeda and, 63, 66; anthrax and, 66, 176; Dark Winter and, 65, 163; future of, 63, 65–67, 161–63; small pox and, 65, 161–63; War on Terror and, 175–76. *See also* terrorism
Black Death, 136
Black Muslim movement, 51
blacks, 50
Blair, Sir Ian, 63
Blair, Tony, 83, 84
Bonaparte, Pauline, 4
Bondevik, Kjell Magne, 53–54
border security: al Qaeda and, 172–73; War on Terror and, 171–74
Borghese Gallery, Italy, 4
Bouyeri, Mohammed, 73
Boyd, Marion, 54
Boyer, Pascal, 159
Britain: Christianity in, 39; Common Law in, 13; demography in, 187; Iraq War and, 84; Muslims in, 51–53, 87; public displays of art in, 1–4, 6–8; radical Islam and, 1–8, 6–8, 55, 81–84; religion in, 155; terrorism in, 69; World War I and, 133–35; World War II and, 22, 107–14
British Advertising Standards Author-

ity, 52

British Common Law, 13

British Muslim Council, 13

Brown v. Board of Education, 122–23

Brussels, Belgium, 7, 18, 19

Brussels Concordance, 20

Buchanan, James, 135

Buchanan, Pat, 81

Budapest, Hungary, 23

Bulgaria, 23

Burnham, James, 101–2

Bush, George W., 81, 91, 109, 136, 150; bin Laden, Osama and, 179; criticism of, 59–61; foreign policy of, 61; War on Terror and, 10, 30, 31, 36–37, 59–61, 137, 165–67

C

California, 8–9, 12

caliphate, 6, 44

Canada, 16, 141; radical Islam in, 54; religion in, 155, 191–92; sharia in, 54

Canova, Antonio, 4

capitalism, 158

Capra, Frank, 115

Catholic Church, 136, 191

CBS, 169

CDC. *See* Centers for Disease Control

censorship, media, 3

Centers for Disease Control (CDC), 161

Cheney, Dick, 164

Chesterton, G. K., 193–94

China, 137–38, 140, 147, 157

Chirac, Jacques, 39, 72, 154

Christian Democratic Union, 75, 83

Christian Social Union, 82

Christianity: in England, 39; in Europe, 90, 152–60; Islamic tolerance and, 6; spread of, 38; in United States, 39

Churchill, Winston: World War I and, 134, 135; World War II and, 98, 108, 111, 112

Cinar, Safter, 83

Civil War, American, 22, 123, 135

Clarke, Richard, 60

Clash of Civilizations, 28, 194

Clinton, Bill, 61

CMCP. *See* Council of Muslim Council Presidents

Cold War, 178, 197

colonialism, 23, 101

Commander in Chief: Franklin Delano Roosevelt, His Lieutenants, and Their War (Larrabee), 113

Communism, 73, 125, 127

Constantinople, 23

Constitution, U.S., 165; First Amendment, 167

Coughlin, Charles, 117

Council of Muslim Council Presidents (CMCP), 20

Council on Foreign Relations, 64

Cromwell, Oliver, 109

The Cube and the Cathedral: Europe, America, and Politics without God (Weigel), 195

D

Danish People's Party, 84

Dante, 135

Dar al–Harb (land of war), 52, 54

Dar al–Sulh (land of truce), 54

Darius, 22

Dark Winter, 65, 163

Darwin's Cathedral (Wilson), 159

Dawson, Christopher, 186

De Imitatione Christi (à Kempis), 136

De Telegraaf, 74

De Volkskrant, 78

Defence of the Realm Act, 108

Defense Department, 178

Democratic Party, Democrats, radical Islam in U.S. and, 9–12

Denmark: immigration and, 84–85; radical Islam and, 84–85, 88

Dennis v. United States, 127–28

Der Spiegel, 74, 75

Die Zeit, 191

discrimination: European Muslims and, 90–91; internment and, 122–23; racial, 122–23; religion and, 90–91

The Disuniting of America (Schlesinger, Jr.), 100

Drudge, Matt, 12

Drudge Report, 13

Dürer, Albrecht, 5

E

Eberstadt, Nicholas, 146

Edmonds, Sibel Dinez, 170

Egypt, 23

Ehrenfeld, Rachel, 169

Ehrlich, Paul, 145

Eid al–Adha (Feast of Sacrifice), 76

Election 2008: American Muslims and, 10–17; media and, 10–11; terrorism and, 17

Eliot, T. S., 194

Eltern, 188

England. *See* Britain

Enlightenment, 26, 102, 157

Espionage Act, 117

d'Estaing, Valéry Giscard, 151

ethnic profiling, 120; War on Terror and, 168–71

EU. *See* European Union

Eurabia, 25, 27, 59, 148, 185

Eurabia: The Euro-Arab Axis (Ye'or), 43

Europe: Age of Discovery in, 23, 135–36; birthrate decline in, 25, 71, 72, 144–45, 185–86; Christianity in, 90, 152–60; demography in, 144–48, 185–89; Eurabia vs., 25, 29, 57, 148, 185; immigration and, 25, 145, 148, 149, 184; Iraq War and, 71, 195; Islamic cultural transformation of, 56, 95–105, 149–52, 190–95; Islamization of, 76; multiculturalism and, 85–87, 93, 186–89; nationalism in, 153–54; political correctness in, 98–105; radical Islam in, 18–20, 21–27, 45–59; religion in, 154–60, 190–92; secularism in, 190–91; social welfare crisis in, 139–40, 192–93; unification of, 71, 88; U.S. alliance with, 20, 27, 39, 184–90, 195–97. *See also* European Muslims; European Union

European Fatwa Council, 54

European Monitoring Centre on Racism and Xenophobia, 89

European Muslims: al Qaeda and, 52; assimilation of, 72; birthrate in Europe and, 71, 72; discrimination and, 90–91; immigration and, 90, 149–51; radical Islam and, 45–59; religion and, 89–90. *See also* American Muslims; Muslims

European Union (EU): France and, 81; immigration and, 20, 149; multiculturalism and, 25–26, 189; political correctness and, 25–26, 99; radical Islam and, 7, 18–20, 56, 71–72; sharia and, 17–18; Turkey and, 71–72, 77, 82, 150, 151, 189–90, 193, 194. *See also* Europe

European Values Study, 153, 155

Eutelsat, 81

F

fascism, 27, 105, 113, 125

Federal Bureau of Investigation (FBI), 110; Arabic translators and, 177; War on Terror and, 170–71; World War II and, 118–19

Federal Emergency Management Agency, 162

Federation of Islamic Organizations in Europe (FIOE), 54

Ferdinand, Archduke, 133–34

Fighting for the Future: Will America Triumph? (Peters), 60

FIOE. *See* Federation of Islamic Organizations in Europe

First Amendment, 167

fitna, 48

Florida, 15

Ford, John, 114–15

Foreign Agents Registration Act of 1938, 118

Fortuyn, Pim, 72, 76

France: border security and, 171–72; demography in, 187; EU and, 81; Iraq War and, 39, 185; public displays of art in, 5; radical Islam and, 5, 7, 70, 79–80; religion in, 155; secularism in, 154–55; terrorism in, 69; World War I and, 26

Francis of Assisi, 135

Frankfurter, Felix, 120, 124–26, 128

Fraser, George MacDonald, 98–99

Frattini, Franco, 149, 150

freedom of speech, 130; wartime restriction of, 123–31

French Enlightenment, 26, 157

French Revolution, 22, 157

Friedman, Thomas, 49

Ft. Minersville School Dist. v. *Gobitis*, 125

Fussell, Paul, 115

G

Gallerie dell'Accademia, Italy, 4

Galloway, George, 83–84

Gallup survey, 155

George VI, 108

Georgia, 65, 161

German-American Bund, 118

Germany: demography in, 187; immigration and, 149–50; Nazism, Nazis in, 47–48, 48–49; radical Islam and, 7, 53, 70, 75–76, 82–83; religion in, 155; terrorism in, 69; World War I and, 133–35

Gingrich, Newt, 35, 36

globalization: international trade and, 140; jihad and, 42–43; radical Islam and, 24; trade and, 140–43; War on Terror and, 182–84
God, 45
Goss, Porter, 63
Great Awakening, 137
Great Depression, 139, 141, 143
Greatest Generation, 113, 173, 197
Greece, 23, 187
Greene, Graham, 194
Grey, Sir Edward, 134
Groves, Leslie, 176
Guardian (London), 51, 55, 81, 159

H

Habsburg, Otto von, 151–52
Hadith, 13
Haider, Jörg, 72
Hamburger Abendblatt, 83
Hand, Learned, 112, 128
Hanseatic League, 136
Harding, Warren, 137
Hart, Gary, 32
Hassan-Shahid, Farzana, 54
Herat, Afghanistan, 64
Hezbollah, 63, 164
Hitler, Adolf, 26, 110, 134; appeasement of, 107; blitzkrieg of, 108; rise of, 22; World War II and, 27–28, 107, 168
Hizb ut-Tahrir al-Islamiyya. *See* Islamic Party of Liberation
Hoagland, Jim, 166
Holland, 25, 54, 57, 69, 74; radical Islam and, 76–79

Hollywood, 15, 115–16
Holocaust, 100
Holmes, Oliver Wendell, 33
Homeland Security Department, 63, 130; border security and, 172; complacency about terrorism and, 8; future terrorist scenarios and, 8, 9; Project BioShield and, 176; radical Islam and, 39
Hoover, J. Edgar, 116
Hughes, Charles Evans, 121
Hundred Years' War, 136
Hungary, 23
Huntington, Samuel, 28
Hussein, Saddam, 84, 137
Hutchinson, Asa, 63, 172

I

immigration: assimilation and, 86; Denmark and, 84–85; EU and, 20, 149; Europe and, 25, 145, 148, 149, 184; European Muslims and, 90, 149–51; Germany and, 149–50; radical Islam and, 80; Sweden and, 80
Imperial Hubris (Scheuer), 59–60
imperialism, 23, 41, 101, 104
In Defense of Internment (Malkin), 121
India, 140, 185
Indians, American, 32–33, 131
Indonesia, 28, 39, 69
infidels, Koran and, 6
Infiltration: How Muslim Spies and Subversives Have Penetrated Washington (Sperry), 170
International Criminal Court, 70

international trade. *See* trade

Internet, 164; Arabic-language websites on, 3, 17; freedom of speech and, 130; jihad and, 42, 49–50; radical Islam and, 2, 4, 6, 24, 29; terrorism and, 2, 4

internment: discrimination and, 122–23; Supreme Court, U.S. and, 119–23, 170; World War II and, 110, 119–23, 170

Interpol, 62, 66

Iran, 30, 137, 147, 164

Iraq, 8, 29; postwar, 63; War on Terror and, 30, 31

Iraq War, 81; Britain and, 84; Europe and, 71, 195; France and, 39

Ireland, 69, 155

Islam: Baptists and, 15; caliphate and, 6, 44; Europeanization of, 76; five pillars of, 42; forced conversion and, 6; jihad and, 41–43; modern, 40–59; pure, 41; Salafi, 40, 43, 92, 166; tolerance and, 6; Wahhabi, 40, 41, 51, 166; West and, 41, 142; women and, 25, 52, 73–74, 79–80. *See also* radical Islam

Islamic Party of Liberation (Hizb ut-Tahrir al-Islamiyya), 44–45

Islamism, 80

Islamization, 43

Islamo-fascism. *See* radical Islam

Islamophobia, 89

Israel, 61, 81, 179–80

Issus, Battle of (333 B.C.), 22

Italy: demography in, 187; future terrorist scenarios in, 4–5; public displays of art in, 4–5; radical Islam in, 4–5; religion in, 155; terrorism in, 69

J

Jackson, Michael, 67

Jackson, Robert, 118, 119

Japanese Americans, 29, 119–23, 147

Jehovah's Witnesses, 124–25

Jesus Christ, 22

Jews: Holocaust and, 100; Islamic tolerance and, 6

jihad: bin Laden, Osama and, 49; globalization and, 42–43; individual, 41–42, 47–48; Internet and, 42, 49–50; Islam and, 41–43; justification for, 41; Koran and, 50; Muslim Brotherhood and, 41; political, 84; radical Islam and, 41–43, 47–50; sharia and, 48; suicide martyrdom and, 42, 49

John III, 96

John Paul II, 191, 195

Johnson v. *Eisentrager*, 119, 120

Judaism, 151

Julliard, Jacques, 80

Justice Department, 118

K

à Kempis, Thomas, 136

Kepel, Gilles, 49–50, 91–92

King, Oona, 83

The Kiss (Rodin), 5

Koran, 37–40, 45, 46; Hadith and, 13; infidels and, 6; jihad and, 50; sharia and, 13; Sunnah and, 13

Kosovo, 23
Kroft, Steve, 169

L

Labour Party (Britain), 83, 84
Larrabee, Eric, 113–14
Latin America, 185
Latinos, 50
Le Figaro, 18, 150
Le Pen, Jean-Marie, 72, 154
Lebanon, 81, 147
Leefbaar Rotterdam (Livable Rotterdam), 76
Leitkultur, 75–76
Lenin, Vladimir, 134
Leno, Jay, 110
Letterman, David, 110
Lewis, C. S., 194
Liberal Party (Denmark), 84
liberalism, 101–2, 124–25
Libya, 147
The Light's on at Signpost (Fraser), 98
Lincoln, Abraham, 33, 125, 135
Lind, William S., 32
Lindh, John Walker, 50
London *Financial Times*, 142
London School of Economics, 3
London *Times*, 52, 79, 80, 82
Louis XVI, 135
Louvre, 5
Loy, James, 172
Lugar, Richard, 66
Luther, Martin, 39

M

MacArthur, Douglas, 198
Macdonald, Ken, 52

Madrid, Spain, train bombings, 73, 82, 85, 104
Maginot Line, 171–72
Magnus, Albertus, 136
Mail on Sunday, 84
Malik, Maleiha, 90–91
Malkin, Michelle, 121
Maloney, William, 107
Malta, 155
Manhattan Project, 176
Manji, Irshad, 45–46
Marcuse, Herbert, 100
Marine Corps Gazette, 32
Marshall, George, 120
Marx, Karl, 158
Marxism, 100, 193
McCollum, Bill, 35
The McLaughlin Group, 164
media: censorship and, 3; Election 2008 and, 10–11; radical Islam and, 2, 3; War on Terror and, 59–61
Medicaid, 129, 140
Medicare, 129, 140
Merkel, Angela, 82–83
Metropolitan Police (England), 2, 4, 63
Mexico, 141, 147, 172
MGM Studios, 115
Michigan, 8–9, 12
Middle East, 28; democracy in, 137, 180; oil in, 70
Midway Island, 114–16
Militant, 117
Milli Gorus, 53
Mineta, Norman, 91, 168–69
modern Islam. *See* Islam; radical Islam

Moldavia, 23

Moore, Michael, 178

Morocco, 147

Mubarak, Hosni, 180

Muggeridge, Malcolm, 194

Muhammad, 41

Muhammad, Omar Bakri, 52–53

Mukhtar, Zahid, 53

multiculturalism: EU and, 25–26, 189; in Europe, 85–87, 93, 186; radical Islam and, 25–26, 74–75, 81, 83, 85, 96–97, 100, 102–3

Musée Auguste Rodin, France, 5

Museo del Prado, Spain, 5

Musharraf, Pervez, 40

Muslim Brotherhood, 41

Muslim Council of Britain, 167

Muslim Parliamentary Association, 167

Muslim Public Affairs Committee, 84

Muslims: assimilation of, 25, 43; British, 51–53, 87; in Canada, 54. *See also* American Muslims; European Muslims

Muslims Against Terrorism, 54

Mustafa, Kara, 96

N

Napoleonic Wars, 57

National Academy of Sciences, 176

National Association of Broadcasters, 116

National Front Party, 154

National Guard, 162

National Public Radio (NPR), 74–75

National Survival Act, 163

nationalism, 26, 153–54

Naumann, Michael, 191–93

Nazism, Nazis, 28, 47–49

Netherlands, 46, 76, 79, 155

New Jersey, 12

New York, 12

New York Times, 49, 74

New Yorker, 108

Newsweek, 164

Nisbet, Robert, 99

Noble, Ronald, 62

Nordio, Mario, 88

North Africa, 147

North Korea, 30

Norway, 7, 53–54, 80

NPR. *See* National Public Radio

nuclear weapons, 64

Nunn, Sam, 163

O

Office of Censorship, 117

Office of Strategic Services (OSS), 114

Ohio, 8–9, 12

Oklahoma, 65, 161

Orwell, George, 133, 160

OSS. *See* Office of Strategic Services

O'Toole, Tara, 65–66

Ottoman Turks, 23–24

Oxford University, 85, 125

P

Pakistan, 39–40, 137, 180

Palestinian Arabs, 70

Panter-Downes, Mollie, 108

Patriot Act, 136

Paul, 39

Pearl Harbor, 107, 118, 121

Pennsylvania, 8–9, 65, 161

people of Islam (ummah), 2

People's Party for Freedom and Democracy, 77

Peregrinus, Petrus, 136

Persian Empire, 22, 23

Peters, Ralph, 60

Philippines, 39

Piccadilly Circus, 1–4, 7–8

Pledge of Allegiance, 124–26, 129

Poland, 155, 187

political correctness: EU and, 25, 99; in Europe, 98–105; response to radical Islam and, 25–26, 98–105; War on Terror and and, 93

Polo, Marco, 135

The Population Bomb (Ehrlich), 145

Powell, Enoch, 72

Press Codes, 117

Princeton University, 85

Project BioShield, 175–76

Promise Keepers, 15

Protestantism, 37

Protestant Reformation, 24, 58

Q

Qutb, Sayyid, 41, 42, 180

R

racism, 101

radical Islam: Belgium and, 7; Britain and, 6–8, 55, 81–82, 83–84; Canada and, 54; change in, 37–40, 40–59; Denmark and, 84–85, 88; deracination of West and, 95–105; economic war and, 139–44; EU and, 7, 18–20, 56; in Europe, 1–8, 18–20, 45–59; European culture and, 1–8, 56, 190–95; European Muslims and, 45–59; European response to, 56–59, 69–93; France and, 5, 7, 79–80; Germany and, 7, 53, 82–83; globalization and, 24; Internet and, 2, 4, 6, 24, 29; Islamic Party of Liberation and, 44; Italy and, 4–5; jihad and, 41–43, 47–50; media and, 2, 3; multiculturalism and, 74–75, 81, 83, 85, 100, 102–3; Netherlands and, 79; Norway and, 7, 53–54; political correctness and, 98–105; recruitment and, 50–51; sharia and, 13–18, 124; Spain and, 5; Sweden and, 80–81; Switzerland and, 7; terrorism and, 38–39; understanding, 28–33, 36–40; United States and, 8–17, 36; War on Terror and, 28–33; World War II and, 27–28; youth and, 48–49. *See also* Islam

Raffarin, Jean-Pierre, 81, 150

Rasmussen, Anders Fogh, 84–85

Reagan, Ronald, 36

Rehnquist, William, 29–30, 31, 111–12

religion: discrimination and, 90–91; European Muslims and, 89–90; race and, 89; secularism vs., 150–51

Republican Party, Republicans: Muslims and, 16; radical Islam in U.S. and, 9–12; September 11, 2001, and, 8; trade and, 141

Reuters, 62

Riksdorfer Elementary School, Germany, 75

Rochefoucauld, Duke de la, 135

Rodin, Auguste, 5

Roe v. *Wade*, 37

Roman law, 111

Romania, 187

Roosevelt, Eleanor, 115

Roosevelt, Franklin D., 111; internment and, 120; investigation of subversion and, 118; liberalism and, 125; Manhattan Project and, 176; media censorship and, 116–18; propaganda and, 115; World War II and, 27–28, 30, 98, 107–8, 112, 114, 185

Roy, Olivier, 40, 42, 44, 45–59

Rudiger, Anja, 89–90

Rumsfeld, Donald, 175

Russia, 64, 185; demography in, 147; Islamic violence in, 38; socialism in, 158

S

Sahlin, Mona, 85–86

Salafist movement, 40, 43, 92, 166

Saudi Arabia, 39, 41, 147, 180

Scheuer, Michael, 24, 59–60

Schilly, Otto, 53, 82

Schlesinger, Arthur, Jr., 100

Schmidt, Helmut, 83

Schönbohm, Jörg, 75

Schröder, Gerhard, 72, 76, 82

science, religion and, 159–60

Second World War. *See* World War II

secularism, 41; in Europe, 190–91; religion vs., 150–51

Senate Foreign Relations Committee, 66

September 11, 2001: impact of, 69; Republican Party and, 8; U.S. response to, 137; U.S. responsibility for, 70; warning signs of, 61

9/11 Commission Report, 177

Serbia, 23

sexism, 101, 104

Shaftesbury, Lord, 7

sharia: American Muslims and, 13–18; British Muslims and, 51; in Canada, 54; EU and, 17–18; jihad and, 48; Koran and, 13; radical Islam and, 13–18, 124

Sicily, 80

Signposts on the Road (Qutb), 41

60 Minutes, 169

Skovgaard-Petersen, Jakob, 88–89

smallpox, 65, 161–63

Smith Act of 1940, 118, 127

Social Justice, 117

Social Security, 140, 141, 188

socialism, 27, 158

Socialist Workers Party (U.S.), 117

Somalia, 39, 73

Sorensen, Ronald, 76

South Carolina, 135

Soviet Union. *See* Russia

Spain: public displays of art in, 5; radical Islam and, 5, 6, 38; terrorism in, 69

Sperry, Paul, 170

"The Spirit of Liberty" (Hand), 112

Stalin, Joseph, 134

State Department, 177

Stevens, George, 115

Stewart, Martha, 67

Stoiber, Edmund, 76, 82, 83

Stone, Harlan Fiske, 121
St. Paul's Cathedral, 18
suicide martyrdom, jihad and, 18, 42
Suicide of the West (Burnham), 101
Sunday Telegraph, 83
Sunnah, 13
Supreme Court, U.S.: free speech restrictions and, 124–30; internment and, 119–23, 170; War on Terror and, 29
Sweden, 80–81
Switzerland, 7
Syria, 23, 147, 164

T

Taliban, 40, 137
Talleyrand, Charles-Maurice de, 71
Tariq ibn Ziyad Islamic center, 76
Tate Modern (England), 3
Terkel, Studs, 113
terrorism: al Qaeda and, 44; bin Laden, Osama and, 63–64; bio-, 63, 65–67, 161–64, 175–76; Election 2008 and, 17; European response to, 69–93; future scenarios of, 1–8; German response to, 75–76; in Holland, 76–79; Internet and, 2, 4; Islamic Party of Liberation and, 44–45; nuclear threat and, 64; radical Islam and, 38–39, 59–67; recruitment and, 50–51; U.S. complacency and, 8; U.S. response to, 9–12; WMD and, 66. *See also* bioterrorism
Thomas Aquinas, 135
Time magazine, 74, 157
Torah, 45

Tory Party (Britain), 83
trade: free, 141; globalization and, 140–43; international, 140–43; Republican Party and, 141
Transylvania, 23
Treasury Department, 117–18
Treaty of Westphalia, 153
Trenton, New Jersey, 12
The Trouble with Islam (Manji), 46
Truman, Harry S., 61, 179
Tunisia, 147
Turkey, 147, 180; EU and, 71–72, 77, 82, 150, 151, 189–90, 193, 194
Turks, Ottoman, 23–24

U

Uffizi museum, Italy, 4
ulema, 48
ummah, 2
United Nations (UN), 31; Iraq War and, 185; Oil for Food program of, 84; world population and, 146, 186–87
United Press International, 192
United States: 1920s in, 138–39; birthrate decline in, 144–45; Black Muslim movement in, 51; border security and, 171–74; Christianity in, 39; demography in, 144–48, 187; EU and, 20; European alliance with, 20, 27, 39, 184–90, 195–97; international trade and, 140–43; Israel and, 179–80; liberalism in, 101–2, 124–25; Protestantism in, 37; radical Islam and, 8–17, 69–71; radical Islam in Europe and, 21; religion in, 156;

social welfare crisis in, 139–40; Taliban and, 40; in World War II, 108, 114–31

U.S. Post Office, 117

U.S. Social Security Trustees, 147

V

van Aartsen, Jozias, 76

van Gogh, Theo, assassination of, 19, 25, 54, 57, 73–76, 78, 79, 81, 85, 95, 104

van Gogh, Vincent, 19, 73

Villepin, Dominique de, 81

Vinson, Frederick Moore, 128

Voorhis Act of 1941, 118

W

Wahhabism, 40, 41, 166

Walachia, 23

War on Terror: Afghanistan and, 30, 31; al Qaeda and, 36–37; Arabic translators and, 177–78; bin Laden, Osama and, 36–37; bioterrorism and, 175–76; border security and, 171–74; Bush, George W. and, 10, 30, 31, 59–61, 137, 165–67; charting progress in, 174–78; Cold War vs., 178; common defense in, 195–97; complacency in, 174–78; Congress and, 31; declaration of war in, 165–68, 179; demography and, 144–48, 185–89; economic war and, 139–44; ethnic profiling and, 168–71; European culture war and, 190–95; fact-based analysis in, 178–82; FBI and, 170; globalization and, 182–84; Iraq and, 30, 31;

media and, 59–61; naming the enemy in, 165–68, 179; national identification cards and, 174; political correctness and, 93; response to radical Islam and, 28–29; targets of, 36; understanding the enemy in, 28–33, 178–79; U.S.-European alliance and, 184–90, 195–97

War Powers Act, 117

Warren, Earl, 120, 123

Washington, George, 180

Washington Post, 107, 166

Washington Times, 78, 172

Waugh, Evelyn, 194

weapons of mass destruction (WMD), 66

Weigel, George, 194–95

West: deracination of, 95–105; Islam and, 21–22, 41, 142; values of, 97–98

Westphalia, Treaty of, 153

Wilders, Geert, 77–79

William of Occam, 136

Wilson, David Sloan, 159

Wilson, Woodrow, 30

WMD. *See* weapons of mass destruction

Wolf, Martin, 142

women: in Catholic Church, 191; honor killings and, 52; Islam and, 25, 52, 73–74, 79–80

Woolsey, James, 163

World Population Prospects (UN), 146

World War I, 30, 57; Britain and, 133–35; France and, 26; free speech restrictions in, 123; nationalism and, 26

World War II, 6, 30, 57; appeasement and, 107; Britain in, 107–14; Churchill, Winston and, 108; England and, 22; fascism and, 105, 113; FBI and, 118–19; free speech restrictions in, 123–31; government intrusions on civil liberties and, 107–31; Hitler, Adolf and, 107, 168; internment and, 110, 119–23, 170; investigation of subversion in, 118–19; Manhattan Project and, 176; media censorship in, 116–18; Midway Island and, 114–16; Pearl Harbor and, 107, 118, 121; propaganda and, 114–16; Roosevelt, Franklin D. and, 107–8, 114, 185; U.S. wartime powers in, 114–31; Western values and, 98
Wren, Sir Christopher, 18

Y

Yemen, 147
Ye'or, Bat, 43
Young, Shelly, 175

Z

ZDF TV, 75
Zubaida, Sami, 87, 89